TABLE OF CONTENTS

HOW TO USE

1

All recipes have yields so please check the number of servings carefully so you don't overeat these snacks.

2

This book is divided into helpful chapters so you can browse the exact type of recipes that you're craving today.

3

There are 78+ recipes in this book, and you can pick and choose whichever snacks fit your mood and lifestyle.

4

Nutritional information (calories, total fat, net carbohydrates, and protein) has been provided for each recipe. Please note that these are just estimates. (Net Carbohydrates = Total Carbohydrates minus Fiber)

THIS BOOK

5

These snacks should not form the basis of your Keto diet! Just remember that these are for when you're traveling, craving something sweet, or having a party.

6

I'm a big fan of batch cooking and cooking in advance. And many of the snacks are great for this...like the Peppermint Patties, Pecan Crisps, and Cajun Roasted Almonds.

7

If you have any questions about the recipes in this cookbook, then please email me at louise@ketosummit.com and I'll try to reply as quickly as possible.

8

Cooking and learning how to heal and nourish your body is all part of the Keto journey. So please enjoy!

EASY, NO-COOK

Idea #1 - Cucumber
Slices/Celery Sticks

Idea #4 - Coconut Butter

Idea #2 -
Canned Tuna

Idea #5 -
100% Chocolate

Idea #3 - Canned
Sardines

Idea #6 - Nuts & Seeds

KETO SNACKS

Idea #7 - Avocado

Idea #10 - Olives

Idea #8 - Beef sticks/
Jerky

Idea #11 - Cacao
Nibs

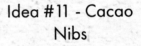

Idea #9 -
Almond Butter

Idea #12 - Smoked Salmon/
Deli Meats

INGREDIENTS

The focus of a good Keto diet is to help nourish your body while keeping your body in ketosis.

Green leafy vegetables, seafoods, fish, meats, and healthy fats should make up the bulk of your diet.

But there are some other ingredients that Keto snacks often use:

ALMOND FLOUR & ALMOND MEAL
Almond flour is very finely ground almonds. You can make your own almond flour by food processing whole almonds into a rough meal.

COCONUT BUTTER
Coconut butter (or coconut manna) is like almond butter but made from shredded coconut.

COCONUT FLOUR
This is finely ground de-fatted dried coconut.

COCONUT MILK
This usually comes in 2 forms, cartons or cans. The canned milk tends to be a lot thicker and higher in fat content. If you refrigerate the cans, the coconut cream rises to the top and can be scooped out. All recipes in this book use the cans.

STEVIA

Stevia is a great Keto sweetener that typically doesn't cause any issues for people. The main downside is that it can leave a bitter aftertaste that some people dislike.

ERYTHRITOL

This is a sugar alcohol that typically causes fewer digestive issues for people. It's great for baking but don't use too much. Try mixing some erythritol with stevia.

FLAX/CHIA SEEDS

Grind these seeds to form a flour/meal that can help stick baked goods together (like eggs do). Best to use a coffee grinder and grind your own as they can go rancid quickly.

MAYO

Most mayos use canola or sunflower or other seed oils that are often rancid and highly processed. But you can make your own by using coconut oil, avocado oil, or olive oil. You can also purchase Paleo mayo in the US.

GHEE

Ghee can be made from butter. It's clarified butter. While we suggest you omit dairy on Keto to maximize your weight loss and health, ghee is typically fine as the milk proteins have been removed. You can make your own by heating butter gently until the milk solids brown and sink.

Is snacking even good on Keto?

As you are probably already aware, snacking can be a bad habit that causes overeating and relies too much on Keto sugars and nuts rather than highly nutritious foods like vegetables, meats, and seafood.

But there are several circumstances when Keto snacks can really help...

1. WHEN YOU'RE HAVING CRAVINGS

Cravings can often catch you unawares. So make sure you have healthy Keto snacks available so that you don't end up eating chocolate bars, cookies, potato chips, and whatever other junk food you might see or have handy.

2. WHEN YOU'RE OUT AND ABOUT

Sometimes you need a snack to keep you going when you're super busy. Keto snacks that you have lying about can be a quick fix to help you move onto the next task.

3. WHEN YOU'RE TRAVELING

Traveling is tough since Keto foods are hard to come by. So packing plenty of delicious Keto snacks will not only keep you full but will also help prevent you from straying.

4. WHEN YOU HAVE PARTIES

Whether you're hosting the party or going to a party, Keto snacks can be great. They're also a helpful way to introduce friends to how easy and tasty Keto can be.

Chapter 1:

CHIPS AND CRACKERS

TORTILLA CHIPS

Prep Time: 5 minutes
Cook Time: 10 minutes
Yield: 2 servings

INGREDIENTS

- 1/3 cup (60 g) chia or flax meal *(use chia or flax seed, and use a coffee grinder or a good blender to process into a flour first)*
- 1/3 cup (40 g) almond flour
- 1 Tablespoon (3 g) Italian seasoning
- 1 teaspoon (5 g) salt
- Water to combine to form a dough *(approx. 2 Tablespoons or 30 ml)*

INSTRUCTIONS

1. Mix all the ingredients together to form a dough.
2. Place the dough on small piece of parchment paper *(so it can fit into the microwave)*. Place another piece of parchment paper on top and use a rolling pin to roll the dough into a thin sheet *(1 mm-thick - it has to be thin so that the microwave can dry it out quickly)*.
3. Remove the top layer of paper and score the dough into triangles *(like chips)* and place the flattened dough with the parchment paper into the microwave for 2 minutes. Check on the chips to make sure they're not burning. Then cook in 1-minute segments until crispy.
4. Alternatively, you can place in a preheated oven at 300°F (150°C) for around 10 minutes *(check oven to make sure the chips don't burn)*.
5. Or, if you have a dehydrator, then dehydrate at a low temperature for approx. 4 hours until crispy.
6. Season with salt and enjoy with one of the dips from this book.

Nutritional Data (estimates) - per serving:
Calories: 121 Fat: 9 g Total Carbs: 8 g Fiber: 5 g Sugar: 0 g
Net Carbs: 3 g Protein: 4 g

ITALIAN FLAXSEED CRACKERS

Prep Time: 15 minutes
Cook Time: 35 minutes
Yield: 4 servings

INGREDIENTS

- 1 cup (120 g) flax seeds, ground into a meal *(use a food processor, blender, or coffee grinder)*
- 1/2 cup (120 ml) water
- 1 Tablespoon (10 g) garlic powder
- 2 teaspoons (5 g) onion powder
- 1 Tablespoon (3 g) Italian seasoning
- 1 teaspoon (5 g) salt

INSTRUCTIONS

1. Preheat oven to 400°F (200°C).
2. In a medium mixing bowl, combine flax meal with all the other dry ingredients. Add water and stir until combined. Knead for a few minutes to form a dough.
3. Place the dough onto a large piece of parchment paper and lay on a flat surface. Place another piece of parchment paper on top of the dough.
4. Use a rolling pin to roll the dough to desired thickness *(approx. 0.3 cm)*.
5. Gently pull the top piece of parchment paper away from the dough. Use a sharp knife or pizza cutter and score the flattened dough into square crackers.
6. Place the parchment paper with the scored dough onto a baking tray and bake for 10-15 minutes *(they should be easy to lift off the parchment paper but not crunchy)*.
7. Carefully pull the crackers apart and flip them over.
8. Reduce oven heat to 300°F (150°C).
9. Bake for another 15-20 minutes until crispy but not burnt.
10. If you have a dehydrator, you can place the crackers in a dehydrator for 6-8 hours on low until they're not soft anymore.

Nutritional Data (estimates) - per serving:
Calories: 151   Fat: 12 g   Total Carbs: 10 g   Fiber: 6 g   Sugar: 1 g
Net Carbs: 4 g   Protein: 6 g

CRUNCHY GARLIC CHIA CRACKERS

Prep Time: 15 minutes
Cook Time: 30 minutes
Yield: 4 servings

INGREDIENTS

- 1/2 cup (60 g) chia or flax meal *(use chia or flax seed, and use a coffee grinder or a good blender to process into a flour first)*
- 1 egg, whisked
- 2 Tablespoons (24 g) chia seeds
- 1 Tablespoon (10 g) garlic powder
- 1 teaspoon (5 g) salt

INSTRUCTIONS

1. Preheat oven to 300°F (150°C).
2. In a mixing bowl, combine all the ingredients.
3. Place a piece of parchment paper on a flat surface. Place the dough on top of the paper and place another piece of parchment paper on top of the dough.
4. Use a rolling pin to roll the dough to desired thickness *(approx. 0.1-0.2 cm thick)*.
5. Carefully pull the top piece of parchment paper away and use a sharp knife to score the dough into small cracker squares.
6. Place the parchment paper with the scored dough on a baking tray and bake for 15 minutes.
7. Break the crackers apart, flip the crackers over, and bake for another 15 minutes. The crackers will get harder after cooling.
8. Enjoy with the **creamy garlic dip** *(see recipe on* ***page 29****)*.

Nutritional Data (estimates) - per serving:
Calories: 123   Fat: 9 g   Total Carbs: 8 g   Fiber: 5 g   Sugar: 1 g
Net Carbs: 3 g   Protein: 6 g

CHEESY KALE CHIPS

Prep Time: 10 minutes
Cook Time: 25 minutes
Yield: 6 servings

INGREDIENTS

- 12 oz (340 g) kale leaves *(with stems on, the bag will weigh around 12 oz but with stems removed, they'll only be 7-8 oz)*
- 1/2 cup (70 g) cashews
- 1/4 cup (32 g) nutritional yeast
- 4 Tablespoons (60 ml) olive oil, divided into two
- Salt and pepper, to taste

INSTRUCTIONS

1. Preheat oven to 300°F (150°C). *(If your oven goes lower, then place it on a lower heat. Or use a dehydrator.)*
2. Remove the stem and pat each kale leaf dry. Toss with 2 tablespoons of olive oil.
3. Place the rest of the ingredients *(cashews, yeast, 2 tablespoons of olive oil, salt and pepper)* into a blender and blend well.
4. Toss with the kale leaves so that the mixture sticks on them.
5. Place kale leaves on large baking trays and bake for 20-25 minutes *(flip after 10 minutes)*. If you're baking at 300°F, then you might want to open the oven door a tiny bit to ensure the kale chips don't burn.

Nutritional Data (estimates) - per serving:
Calories: *177* Fat: *14 g* Total Carbs: *9 g* Fiber: *3 g* Sugar: *2 g*
Net Carbs: *6 g* Protein: *6 g*

EASY ZUCCHINI CHIPS

Prep Time: 2 minutes
Cook Time: 1 hour
Yield: 4 servings

INGREDIENTS

- 1 zucchini, very thinly sliced *(use a mandolin, if possible)*
- 2 Tablespoons (30 ml) olive oil
- 1/4 teaspoon (1 g) salt

INSTRUCTIONS

1. Preheat oven to 300°F (150°C). *(If your oven goes lower, then place it on a lower heat. Or use a dehydrator.)*
2. Pat the zucchini slices very dry using a paper towel to soak up excess water.
3. Toss the slices with the olive oil and salt.
4. Place on a large parchment paper-lined baking tray and bake for 1 hour *(it may need to be longer if you used a much lower oven temperature or a dehydrator)* until the chips are crispy.

Nutritional Data (estimates) - per serving:
Calories: 64 Fat: 7 g Total Carbs: 1 g Fiber: 0 g Sugar: 1 g
Net Carbs: 1 g Protein: 0 g

PEPPERONI CHIPS

Prep Time: 5 minutes
Cook Time: 15 minutes
Yield: 4 servings

INGREDIENTS

- 1 (8 oz or 225 g) package pepperoni, thin sliced

INSTRUCTIONS

1. Preheat oven to 350°F (175°C).
2. Place a piece of parchment paper on the baking sheet and lay each pepperoni slice on the parchment paper so they don't overlap.
3. Bake for 10-15 minutes until they're crispy *(they'll get crispier as they cool)*.
4. Lay a few layers of paper towels on a plate and place the baked pepperoni chips on top to soak up some of the excess fat.

Nutritional Data (estimates) - per serving:
Calories: 276 Fat: 24 g Total Carbs: 0 g Fiber: 0 g Sugar: 0 g
Net Carbs: 0 g Protein: 12 g

PAPRIKA LIME GREEN BEAN FRIES

Prep Time: 10 minutes
Cook Time: 25 minutes
Yield: 4 servings

INGREDIENTS

- 1/2 lb (225 g) green beans, cut into half
- 1 egg, whisked
- 1/2 cup (60 g) almond flour or any nut flour of your choice
- 1 Tablespoon (6 g) paprika
- Zest of 1 lime
- Salt and pepper, to taste

INSTRUCTIONS

1. Preheat oven to 350°F (175°C).
2. Combine the dry ingredients (almond flour, paprika, lime zest, salt, and pepper) together.
3. Dredge the green beans in the whisked egg first then generously coat with the dry mixture. It can be a bit hard to stick so press the mixture on well.
4. Place individually on a parchment paper-lined baking sheet and bake for 20-25 minutes until golden. (Note - these are not crispy fries.)

Nutritional Data (estimates) - per serving:
Calories: 107 Fat: 7 g Total Carbs: 7 g Fiber: 4 g Sugar: 1 g
Net Carbs: 3 g Protein: 6 g

TOASTED COCONUT FLAKES

Prep Time: 5 minutes
Cook Time: 7 minutes
Yield: 4 servings

INGREDIENTS

- 2 Tablespoons (30 ml) coconut oil, slightly melted
- 1 cup (60 g) coconut flakes
- 2 Tablespoons (24 g) erythritol or stevia, to taste *(optional)*
- Dash of salt

INSTRUCTIONS

1. Preheat oven to 300°F (150°C).
2. Mix the coconut flakes in the coconut oil, sweetener, and salt.
3. Place on a parchment paper-lined baking tray.
4. Bake for 6-7 minutes. Remove quickly as it burns fast.
5. Let cool and enjoy.

Nutritional Data (estimates) - per serving:
Calories: 172 Fat: 17 g Total Carbs: 6 g Fiber: 3 g Sugar: 1 g
Net Carbs: 3 g Protein: 2 g

Chapter 2:

DIPS

"HUMMUS" WITH CAULIFLOWER AND TAHINI

Prep Time: 10 minutes
Cook Time: 10 minutes
Yield: 4 servings

INGREDIENTS

- 1/2 head (approx. 11 oz or 300 g) cauliflower, broken into florets
- 3 Tablespoons (45 ml) **keto mayo** *(see recipe on **page 32**)*
- 3 cloves of garlic, peeled
- 2 Tablespoons (30 ml) lemon juice
- 1 Tablespoon (15 ml) white tahini *(sesame seed paste)*
- Sea salt and freshly ground black pepper, to taste

INSTRUCTIONS

1. Steam the cauliflower until softened. Drain the water well.
2. Place steamed cauliflower into a blender and blend really well with the rest of the ingredients.

Nutritional Data (estimates) - per serving: Does not include celery or carrot sticks
Calories: 124   Fat: 11 g   Total Carbs: 6 g   Fiber: 2 g   Sugar: 2 g   Net Carbs: 4 g
Protein: 2 g

CREAMY GARLIC DIP

Prep Time: 5 minutes
Cook Time: 0 minutes
Yield: 4 servings

INGREDIENTS
- 10 cloves of garlic, peeled
- 1/4 cup (60 ml) olive oil
- 2 teaspoons (10 ml) lemon juice
- 2 Tablespoons (30 ml) **keto mayo** *(see recipe on __page 32__)*
- Dash of salt

INSTRUCTIONS
1. Blend all the ingredients together well.

Nutritional Data (estimates) - per serving:
Calories: 179   Fat: 20 g   Total Carbs: 3 g   Fiber: 0 g   Sugar: 0 g   Net Carbs: 3 g
Protein: 0 g

GUACAMOLE

Prep Time: 10 minutes
Cook Time: 0 minutes
Yield: 2 servings

INGREDIENTS

- 1 medium ripe avocado, stone removed
- 1/2 teaspoon (3 ml) lime juice
- 1/2 teaspoon (1 g) onion powder
- 1/2 teaspoon (2 g) garlic powder
- Chili powder, to taste *(if you want it spicy)*
- 2 cherry tomatoes, finely chopped
- 1 Tablespoon (2 g) cilantro chopped *(or 1 teaspoon (1 g) dried cilantro)*
- Salt, to taste

INSTRUCTIONS

1. Mash the avocado in a bowl and add in the lime juice.
2. Add in the onion powder, garlic powder, chili powder *(optional)*, cilantro, and diced cherry tomatoes and mix well.
3. Add salt to taste and serve.

Nutritional Data (estimates) - per serving:
Calories: 300   Fat: 25 g   Total Carbs: 19 g   Fiber: 14 g   Sugar: 3 g
Net Carbs: 5 g   Protein: 4 g

KETO MAYO

Prep Time: 15 minutes
Cook Time: 0 minutes
Yield: 16 servings

INGREDIENTS

- 1 egg
- 1 Tablespoon (15 ml) apple cider vinegar
- 1 cup (240 ml) olive oil or avocado oil

INSTRUCTIONS

Using a regular blender -

1. Add the egg to the vinegar and blend together.
2. Then keep blending and add in the avocado oil slowly. You'll hear the blender sound change when you've added in enough avocado oil and the mixture will thicken all of a sudden.
3. Store in the fridge and use in under a week.

Using an immersion blender -

1. Add all the ingredients into a tall container.
2. Place the immersion blender all the way to the bottom of the container before turning it on.
3. Blend with the immersion blender at the bottom of the container for 10 seconds.
4. Then move the immersion blender up and down to combine everything.

Nutritional Data (estimates) - per serving:
Calories: 100   Fat: 12 g   Total Carbs: 0g   Fiber: 0 g   Sugar: 0 g   Net Carbs: 0 g
Protein: 0 g

HAWAIIAN "HUMMUS"

Prep Time: 5 minutes
Cook Time: 0 minutes
Yield: 4 servings

INGREDIENTS
- 1 cup (128 g) macadamia nuts
- 3 Tablespoons (45 ml) lemon juice
- 3 cloves of garlic, peeled
- 2 Tablespoons (30 ml) avocado oil, to get it blending (add more if needed)
- Salt and pepper, to taste

INSTRUCTIONS
1. Place all ingredients into a food processor or blender and blend until smooth.

Nutritional Data (estimates) - per serving:
Calories: 306   Fat: 31 g   Total Carbs: 6 g   Fiber: 4 g   Sugar: 1 g   Net Carbs: 2 g
Protein: 3 g

ROASTED CAULIFLOWER DIP

Prep Time: 10 minutes
Cook Time: 30 minutes
Yield: 2 servings

INGREDIENTS

- 1/2 head (approx. 11 oz or 300 g) cauliflower, broken into florets
- 3 Tablespoons (45 ml) olive oil, divided
- 3 cloves of garlic, peeled
- 2 Tablespoons (30 ml) lemon juice
- 2 teaspoons (10 ml) almond butter
- Sea salt and freshly ground black pepper, to taste
- 1 teaspoon (2 g) fresh parsley, finely chopped
- Cherry tomatoes and cucumber batons, to serve with

INSTRUCTIONS

1. Preheat oven to 400°F (200°C).
2. Toss the cauliflower florets in 2 tablespoons of olive oil.
3. Spread the cauliflower florets out on a greased baking tray. Take the garlic cloves as they are and secure inside a small foil parcel where no air can escape. Place onto the same tray. Roast both the garlic and cauliflower in the oven for 30 minutes, tossing the cauliflower after 15 minutes to ensure even roasting.
4. Remove the roasted cauliflower from the oven *(which should have completely softened)* and unwrap the garlic. Place both into a mini food processor. Add the lemon juice *(check for pips)*, the almond butter, and the additional tablespoon of olive oil and blend the mixture to a smooth puree.
5. Season with salt and pepper to your liking. Top with parsley and serve with cherry tomatoes and cucumber batons, or any other vegetables that your daily macros will allow.

Nutritional Data (estimates) - per serving:
Calories: 249   Fat: 24 g   Total Carbs: 10 g   Fiber: 4 g   Sugar: 4 g
Net Carbs: 6 g   Protein: 4 g

ROASTED EGGPLANT DIP

Prep Time: 10 minutes
Cook Time: 40 minutes
Yield: 6 servings

INGREDIENTS

- 1 large eggplant *(approx. 1 lb or 450 g)*
- 4 cloves of garlic, peeled
- 2 Tablespoons (30 ml) fresh lemon juice
- 1 Tablespoon (15 ml) coconut cream *(from the top of refrigerated cans of coconut milk)*
- 1 Tablespoon (15 ml) tahini paste
- Salt and pepper, to taste
- 1 teaspoon (3 g) sesame seeds, for garnish

INSTRUCTIONS

1. Preheat oven to 400°F (200°C).
2. Prick the eggplant a few times with a fork. Then place on a baking tray and roast for 30-40 minutes until tender.
3. If you want a smoky flavor, then place the eggplant under the broiler for a few minutes to blacken the skin a bit.
4. Let the eggplant cool, then cut in half and scoop out the flesh.
5. Blend the eggplant flesh with the garlic, lemon juice, coconut cream, tahini paste, salt and pepper. Adjust seasoning to taste.
6. Spoon into a bowl and sprinkle with sesame seeds for garnish.

Nutritional Data (estimates) - per serving:
Calories: 45   Fat: 2 g   Total Carbs: 6 g   Fiber: 3 g   Sugar: 2 g   Net Carbs: 3 g
Protein: 1 g

HERB RANCH DIP

Prep Time: 5 minutes
Cook Time: 0 minutes
Yield: 4 servings

INGREDIENTS

- 1/4 cup (60 ml) **keto mayo** *(see recipe on __page 32__)*
- 1/4 cup (60 ml) coconut cream *(from the top of refrigerated cans of coconut milk)*
- 1 teaspoon (5 ml) lemon juice
- 1 clove of garlic, peeled and finely diced
- 1/2 teaspoon (1 g) onion powder
- 1 Tablespoon (2 g) fresh parsley, finely chopped *(or 1 teaspoon dried parsley)*
- 1 Tablespoon (2 g) fresh chives, finely chopped *(or omit)*
- 1 teaspoon (1 g) fresh dill, finely chopped *(or 1/2 teaspoon (0.5 g) dried dill)*
- Dash of salt
- Dash of pepper

INSTRUCTIONS

1. Mix together the keto mayo, coconut cream, lemon juice, onion powder, salt, and pepper with a fork.
2. Gently fold in the finely diced garlic and fresh herbs.

Nutritional Data (estimates) - per serving:
Calories: 131   Fat: 15 g   Total Carbs: 1 g   Fiber: 0 g   Sugar: 0 g   Net Carbs: 1 g
Protein: 0 g

BUFFALO CHICKEN DIP

Prep Time: 10 minutes
Cook Time: 30 minutes
Yield: 8 servings

INGREDIENTS

- 2 chicken breasts (approx. 1 lb or 450 g), diced and sauteed in coconut oil *(or 3 cups of cooked chicken meat)*
- 1 cup (240 ml) **keto mayo** *(see recipe on **page 32**)*
- 1/3 cup (80 ml) hot sauce *(adjust if you don't want it as spicy)*
- 2 Tablespoons (30 ml) mustard
- 1 Tablespoon (7 g) onion powder
- 1 Tablespoon (10 g) garlic powder
- Salt and pepper, to taste

INSTRUCTIONS

1. Preheat oven to 350°F (175°C).
2. Shred the cooked chicken and mix with the rest of the ingredients. *(Cook the chicken first if you don't have cooked chicken available.)*
3. Pour the mixture into a small casserole dish *(or 8-by-8 inch pan)* and bake for 25-30 minutes until bubbling.

Nutritional Data (estimates) - per serving:
Calories: 404   Fat: 39 g   Total Carbs: 2 g   Fiber: 0 g   Sugar: 1 g   Net Carbs: 2 g
Protein: 16 g

FAUX FRENCH ONION DIP

Prep Time: 10 minutes
Cook Time: 5 minutes
Yield: 4 servings

INGREDIENTS
- 1/2 onion, diced
- 2 Tablespoons (30 ml) avocado oil, to cook onions with
- 1/2 cup (120 ml) **keto mayo** (see recipe on _page 32_)
- 1 Tablespoon (10 g) garlic powder or 2 cloves of garlic, finely chopped
- 1 Tablespoon (7 g) dried onion flakes
- 1 Tablespoon (3 g) dried parsley
- Salt and pepper, to taste

INSTRUCTIONS
1. Heat the avocado oil in a hot frying pan. Add the diced onion to the pan and fry until slightly browned.
2. Place the onions on a plate and let cool for 5 minutes.
3. Mix everything together and season with salt and pepper, to taste.

Nutritional Data (estimates) - per serving:
Calories: 278   Fat: 31 g   Total Carbs: 4 g   Fiber: 1 g   Sugar: 2 g   Net Carbs: 3 g
Protein: 0 g

SPINACH ARTICHOKE DIP

Prep Time: 10 minutes
Cook Time: 0 minutes
Yield: 12 servings

INGREDIENTS

- 10 oz (283 g) frozen chopped spinach, defrosted
- 14 oz (400 g) artichoke hearts (from can in water), drained and chopped
- 3/4 cup (180 ml) **keto mayo** *(see recipe on **page 32**)*
- 1/2 cup (120 ml) cashew cheese
- 1/2 onion, diced
- 4 cloves of garlic, peeled and minced
- 2 teaspoons (10 ml) lemon juice
- Salt and pepper, to taste

INSTRUCTIONS

1. Drain the spinach and artichoke well. Make sure the spinach, artichoke, and onions are finely chopped.
2. In a large bowl, mix everything together well.
3. Season with salt and pepper, to taste.
4. Serve hot or cold with some **tortilla chips** *(see recipe on **page 13**)*.

Nutritional Data (estimates) - per serving:
Calories: 144   Fat: 14 g   Total Carbs: 5 g   Fiber: 2 g   Sugar: 1 g   Net Carbs: 3 g
Protein: 2 g

ONIONS AND CHIVES CASHEW CHEESE DIP

Prep Time: 10 minutes
Cook Time: 0 minutes
Yield: 12 servings
Serving size: 3 Tablespoons

INGREDIENTS

- 1 cup (4 oz or 120 g) raw cashews
- 1/4 cup (60 ml) coconut oil
- 1/4 cup (60 ml) water
- 1 teaspoon (3 g) garlic powder
- 2 Tablespoons (16 g) nutritional yeast
- 1/4 onion, finely chopped
- 1 Tablespoon chives, finely chopped
- Dash of salt

INSTRUCTIONS

1. Place the raw cashews into a bowl of room temperature water so that it covers the cashews, drape a paper towel or tea towel over the bowl to prevent dust settling, and soak overnight. Drain well before using.
2. Place the soaked cashews, 1/4 cup fresh water, salt, garlic powder, nutritional yeast, and coconut oil into a blender and blend until smooth.
3. Stir in the finely chopped onions and chives.

Nutritional Data (estimates) - per serving:
Calories: 97   Fat: 9 g   Total Carbs: 4 g   Fiber: 1 g   Sugar: 1 g   Net Carbs: 3 g
Protein: 2 g

COCONUT NUTELLA

Prep Time: 10 minutes
Cook Time: 10 minutes
Yield: 16 servings
Serving size: 2 Tablespoons

INGREDIENTS

- 2 cups (250 g) whole, raw hazelnuts
- 6 Tablespoons (36 g) raw cacao powder
- 2 Tablespoons (30 ml) MCT or coconut oil, divided
- 1/2 cup (120 ml) full-fat canned coconut milk
- 1 teaspoon (5 ml) pure vanilla extract
- Erythritol and stevia, to taste
- Dash of salt

INSTRUCTIONS

1. Preheat oven to 325°F (160°C).
2. Place the raw hazelnuts on a baking tray and roast in the preheated oven for 10 minutes. You want the skins dark brown but not burnt. Remove from the oven, and when cool enough to handle, dampen some paper towels and rub the skins off.
3. Blend the nuts and 1 Tablespoon of the MCT oil into a butter using a high-speed blender. Add the remaining ingredients and blend into a creamy Nutella consistency.

Nutritional Data (estimates) - per serving:
*Calories: 157 Fat: 15 g Total Carbs: 3 g Fiber: 3 g Sugar: 0 g Net Carbs: 0 g
Protein: 2 g*

Chapter 3:

BAKED GOODS

BLUEBERRY MUFFINS

Prep Time: 10 minutes
Cook Time: 20 minutes
Yield: 6 muffins

INGREDIENTS

- 1 1/2 cups (180 g) almond flour
- 1/4 cup (60 ml) ghee, melted but not too hot
- 2 eggs, whisked
- 1 Tablespoon (15 ml) vanilla extract
- Erythritol or stevia, to taste
- 1/2 teaspoon (4 g) baking soda
- Dash of salt
- Approx. 24 blueberries (1/2 cup), divided

INSTRUCTIONS

1. Preheat oven to 350°F (175°C).
2. Melt the ghee in a mixing bowl. Add in the almond flour, eggs, vanilla extract, sweetener, baking soda, and salt. Mix everything together well.
3. Break up the blueberries gently by poking with a sharp knife to burst the skin. Stir half of the blueberries into the mixture.
4. Save 12 blueberries to put on top near the end.
5. Line a muffin pan with muffin liners or grease it. Spoon the mixture into the muffin pan *(to around 3/4 full)*. Makes 6 muffins. Place 2 blueberries at the top of each muffin.
6. Bake for 18-20 minutes until a toothpick comes out clean when you insert it into a muffin.

Nutritional Data (estimates) - per muffin:
Calories: 240   Fat: 22 g   Total Carbs: 6 g   Fiber: 3 g   Sugar: 2 g   Net Carbs: 3 g
Protein: 7 g

ALMOND FLOUR COOKIES WITH LEMON ZEST

Prep Time: 10 minutes
Cooking Time: 20 minutes
Yield: 4 servings

INGREDIENTS

- 1 cup (120 g) almond flour
- 1 egg, whisked
- 3 Tablespoons (45 ml) ghee, melted
- Erythritol or stevia, to taste
- 1 teaspoon (5 ml) vanilla extract
- 1 Tablespoon lemon zest
- 1/2 teaspoon (2 ml) lemon extract
- Pinch of (1 g) baking soda

INSTRUCTIONS

1. Preheat oven to 350°F (175°C).
2. Mix all the ingredients together in a mixing bowl to form a dough.
3. Chill the dough for 20 minutes in the fridge.
4. Using a stencil or cookie cutter, or just your hands, form the dough into 8 small round cookies.
5. Place on a parchment paper-lined baking tray.
6. Bake for 15-20 minutes until the cookies are slightly browned.
7. Remove from oven and place on a cooling rack. They'll crisp up after cooling.

Nutritional Data (estimates) - per serving:
Calories: 242   Fat: 23 g   Total Carbs: 5 g   Fiber: 3 g   Sugar: 1 g   Net Carbs: 2 g
Protein: 7 g

CARROT CAKE

Prep Time: 20 minutes
Cook Time: 30 minutes
Yield: 16 slices

INGREDIENTS

For the cake layers -
- 5 medium eggs
- 3/4 cup (144 g) erythritol
- 3 carrots (150 g), shredded and liquid squeezed out
- 2 teaspoons (10 ml) of vanilla extract
- 1 1/2 cups (180 g) of almond flour
- 1/4 cup (28 g) flax meal (*use a food processor, blender, or coffee grinder to grind flax seeds into flax meal*)
- 1/4 cup (20 g) shredded coconut
- 1/2 cup (56 g) coconut flour
- 1/2 cup (59 g) walnuts, chopped
- 3/4 cup (180 ml) ghee or coconut oil
- 2 teaspoons (4 g) baking powder
- 2 teaspoons (4 g) of cinnamon powder
- 1 teaspoon (2 g) of ginger powder
- 1 Tablespoon (15 ml) apple cider vinegar
- Dash of nutmeg
- Dash of salt

For the frosting -
- 1 cup (240 ml) coconut butter (*+ coconut oil if needed*)
- 1/4 cup erythritol or stevia (*or to taste*)
- 1/2 teaspoon (3 ml) vanilla extract
- Dash of salt

INSTRUCTIONS

1. Preheat oven to 350°F (175°C).
2. In a large mixing bowl, whisk together the ingredients for the cake layers.
3. Line two 9-inch (23 cm) cake pans with parchment paper (*make sure to line both the base and sides of the pan*).
4. Divide the cake batter between the 2 pans and bake in preheated oven for 30 minutes.
5. Check the cake is done by inserting a cocktail stick and making sure it comes out clean.
6. Meanwhile whip together the frosting ingredients.
7. Spread half of the frosting onto one of the cake layers, then place the other on top and spread the rest of the frosting on top.

Nutritional Data (estimates) - per serving:
Calories: 322   Fat: 30 g   Total Carbs: 9 g   Fiber: 3 g   Sugar: 2 g   Net Carbs: 3 g
Protein: 6 g

SNICKERDOODLES

Prep Time: 10 minutes
Cooking Time: 10 minutes
Yield: 20 servings

INGREDIENTS

For the cookies -
- 1 cup (120 g) almond flour
- 2 Tablespoons (14 g) flax meal *(use a food processor, blender, or coffee grinder to grind flax seeds into flax meal)*
- 1/2 cup (120 ml) ghee
- 1/3-1/2 cup (64 - 96 g) erythritol
- 1 egg, whisked
- 1 teaspoon (4 g) baking soda
- 1 teaspoon (2 g) baking powder
- 1 teaspoon (5 ml) vanilla extract
- Dash of salt

For the cinnamon sugar -
- 2 Tablespoons (24 g) erythritol
- 1 Tablespoon (6 g) cinnamon powder

INSTRUCTIONS

1. Preheat oven to 350°F (175°C).
2. Mix all the cookie ingredients together in a bowl until a soft dough forms. Place into the fridge for 30 minutes.
3. In a separate bowl, mix together the cinnamon sugar ingredients.
4. Form small balls from the dough and dip into the cinnamon sugar. Press into a round cookie and place onto a parchment paper-lined baking tray. The cookies spread so make sure to leave enough room between the cookies.
5. Bake for 5-7 minutes *(the cinnamon burns quickly)*.

Nutritional Data (estimates) - per cookie:
Calories: 82   Fat: 8 g   Total Carbs: 1 g   Fiber: 1 g   Sugar: 0 g   Net Carbs: 0 g
Protein: 1 g

"CORNBREAD" MUFFINS

Prep Time: 10 minutes
Cook Time: 20 minutes
Yield: 6 muffins

INGREDIENTS

- 3/4 cup (90 g) almond flour
- 1/4 cup (30 g) coconut flour
- 2 teaspoons (9 g) baking powder
- 1 teaspoon (5 g) salt
- 2 Tablespoons (30 ml) ghee, melted but not too hot
- 3 eggs, whisked
- 1/2 cup (120 ml) coconut milk
- 1 Tablespoon (12 g) erythritol or stevia, to taste

INSTRUCTIONS

1. Preheat oven to 350°F (175°C).
2. Grease muffin pan or use muffin liners or silicone muffin pan.
3. Mix together all ingredients well in a large bowl.
4. Pour the batter into the muffin pan *(makes 6 muffins)*.
5. Bake for 18-20 minutes until a toothpick comes out clean when you insert it into a muffin.

Nutritional Data (estimates) - per muffin:
Calories: 191   Fat: 17 g   Total Carbs: 5 g   Fiber: 3 g   Sugar: 1 g   Net Carbs: 2 g
Protein: 6 g

GINGER COCONUT COOKIES

Prep Time: 10 minutes
Cook Time: 20 minutes
Yield: 4 servings

INGREDIENTS

- 2/3 cup (80 g) almond meal
- 1/4 cup (28 g) coconut flour
- 2 Tablespoons (10 g) coconut flakes
- 1 egg, whisked
- 3 Tablespoons (45 ml) ghee, melted
- Erythritol or stevia, to taste
- 1 teaspoon (5 ml) vanilla extract
- 2 teaspoons (4 g) ginger powder
- Pinch of (1 g) baking soda

INSTRUCTIONS

1. Preheat oven to 350°F (175°C).
2. Combine all the ingredients in a mixing bowl to form a dough.
3. If you have time, place the dough in the fridge for 15-20 minutes to chill.
4. Then using a cookie cutter, form small cookies *(approx. 8 cookies)*.
5. Place on a baking tray and bake for 15-20 minutes until they are just slightly browned on top.
6. Remove from oven and place on a cooling rack.

Nutritional Data (estimates) - per serving:
Calories: 237   Fat: 21 g   Total Carbs: 7 g   Fiber: 5 g   Sugar: 1 g   Net Carbs: 2 g
Protein: 6 g

CHOCOLATE BROWNIES

Prep Time: 10 minutes
Cook Time: 15 minutes
Yield: 9 servings

INGREDIENTS

- 6 Tablespoons (90 ml) coconut oil or ghee, melted but not too hot
- 3 eggs, whisked
- 2 teaspoons (10 ml) vanilla extract
- 1 cup (120 g) almond flour
- 1 cup (80 g) unsweetened cacao powder
- 2 Tablespoons (30 ml) coconut cream *(from the top of refrigerated cans of coconut milk)*
- 1/2 cup (96 g) granulated erythritol or stevia, to taste

INSTRUCTIONS

1. Preheat the oven to 350°F (175°C).
2. Whisk the eggs well, then stir in the vanilla extract, coconut cream and coconut oil *(ensuring the coconut oil is not too hot, else it will scramble the eggs)*. Mix well and set aside.
3. Combine the almond flour, unsweetened cacao powder, and sweetener in a bowl.
4. Add the wet egg mixture to the almond flour mixture and combine until fully incorporated.
5. Tip the mixture into a small, greased baking dish *(approx. 8-inch or 20 cm square)*, smooth down the top and place in the oven for 15 minutes.
6. Use a cake tester to ensure the brownies have cooked, then remove and allow to cool before slicing into 9 squares.

Nutritional Data (estimates) - per serving:
Calories: 210   Fat: 18 g   Total Carbs: 8 g   Fiber: 5 g   Sugar: 1 g   Net Carbs: 3 g
Protein: 7 g

CHOCOLATE CHIP SNACK CAKE

Prep Time: 10 minutes
Cook Time: 30 minutes
Yield: 2 servings

INGREDIENTS

- 3/4 cup (90 g) almond flour
- 2 Tablespoons (24 g) granulated erythritol
- 2 Tablespoons (20 g) 100% dark chocolate chips
- 1/2 teaspoon (1 g) baking powder
- 1 medium egg, lightly whisked
- 2 Tablespoons (30 ml) coconut oil, melted and cooled (*plus additional to grease ramekin*)
- 1 Tablespoon (15 ml) unsweetened almond milk
- 1 teaspoon (5 ml) vanilla extract

INSTRUCTIONS

1. Preheat the oven to 350°F (175°C). Grease a ramekin with coconut oil and set aside.
2. In a medium bowl, whisk to combine all of the ingredients until smooth. Pour the batter into the prepared ramekin.
3. Place the ramekin in the oven and bake for 25 to 30 minutes until cooked through and a toothpick inserted into the center comes out clean. (*Check the cake after 15 minutes and cover with aluminum foil for the remaining cook time if the top of the loaf is browning too quickly.*)
4. Remove from the oven and let cool for 10 minutes before removing the cake from the ramekin.
5. If desired, serve slightly warm for gooey chocolate or allow the cake to cool completely before serving.

Nutritional Data (estimates) - per serving:
Calories: 298   Fat: 23 g   Total Carbs: 9 g   Fiber: 5 g   Sugar: 2 g
Net Carbs: 4 g   Protein: 12 g

RASPBERRY LEMON MUFFINS

Prep Time: 10 minutes
Cook Time: 20 minutes
Yield: 12 muffins

INGREDIENTS
- 3 cups (360 g) almond flour
- 1/2 cup (120 ml) ghee or coconut oil, melted but not too hot
- 4 eggs, whisked
- 1 cup raspberries (68 g)
- 2 Tablespoons (12 g) lemon zest
- 1 Tablespoon (15 ml) vanilla extract
- 1/4 cup (48 g) erythritol or stevia, to taste
- 1 teaspoon (4 g) baking soda

INSTRUCTIONS
1. Preheat oven to 350°F (175°C).
2. Mix together all the ingredients in a large mixing bowl.
3. Pour into muffin pans (use silicone muffin pans or grease the metal pans). Makes 12 muffins.
4. Bake for 18-20 minutes until a toothpick comes out clean when you insert it into a muffin.

Nutritional Data (estimates) - per serving:
Calories: 258 Fat: 22 g Total Carbs: 10 g Fiber: 6 g Sugar: 3 g
Net Carbs: 4 g Protein: 7 g

CINNAMON DONUT BALLS

Prep Time: 10 minutes
Cook Time: 15 minutes
Yield: 6 servings

INGREDIENTS
- 1 cup (120 g) almond flour
- 1/4 cup (48 g) granulated erythritol or stevia, to taste
- 1 egg, whisked
- 2 Tablespoons (30 ml) ghee, melted but not hot
- 1 teaspoon (4 g) baking powder
- 2 Tablespoons (14 g) cinnamon
- 1 teaspoon (2 g) ginger powder

INSTRUCTIONS
1. Preheat oven to 350°F (175°C).
2. Combine all the ingredients together in a mixing bowl.
3. Form 12 balls from the dough.
4. Place on a piece of parchment paper and bake for 15 minutes.

Nutritional Data (estimates) - per serving:
Calories: 148   Fat: 13 g   Total Carbs: 5 g   Fiber: 3 g   Sugar: 1 g   Net Carbs: 2 g
Protein: 4 g

RED VELVET CUPCAKES

Prep Time: 15 minutes
Cook Time: 25-30 minutes
Yield: 12 cupcakes

INGREDIENTS

For the cupcakes -
- 1 cup (120 g) almond flour
- 1/2 cup (120 ml) coconut oil
- 3 Tablespoons (45 ml) apple cider vinegar
- 3 eggs, whisked
- 1 beet, raw, peeled and diced
- Sweetener, to taste
- 4 Tablespoons (24 g) unsweetened cacao powder
- 2 teaspoons (8 g) baking soda
- 1 teaspoon (4 g) baking powder
- 1 Tablespoon (15 ml) of vanilla extract
- Dash of salt

For the frosting -
- 1/4 cup (60 ml) cashew cheese
- 2 Tablespoons (30 ml) coconut cream
- 2 Tablespoons (30 ml) coconut oil
- Erythritol or stevia *(or to taste)*
- 1/2 teaspoon (3 ml) vanilla extract
- Dash of salt

INSTRUCTIONS

1. Preheat oven to 350°F (175°C).
2. Puree the beet and add in the vinegar and coconut oil. Add in the other ingredients and blend well.
3. Divide between 12 muffin pans.
4. Bake for 25-30 minutes until a toothpick comes out clean.
5. Meanwhile make the frosting by blending all the ingredients together. Spread on top of the cupcakes once they're cooled.

Nutritional Data (estimates) - per serving:
Calories: 189   Fat: 18 g   Total Carbs: 4 g   Fiber: 2 g   Sugar: 1 g   Net Carbs: 2 g
Protein: 4 g

CINNAMON ROLLS

Prep Time: 90 minutes
Cook Time: 20 minutes
Yield: 8 cinnamon rolls

INGREDIENTS

- 2 Tablespoons (30 g) sugar*
- 1/4 cup (60 ml) ghee, melted
- 3/4 cup (180 ml) unsweetened almond milk
- 1 Tablespoon (8.5 g) active dry yeast

For the dough -

- 1 Tablespoon (15 ml) apple cider vinegar
- 1 cup (120 g) almond flour
- 1 cup (112 g) coconut flour
- 2 Tablespoons (20 g) collagen powder
- 2 teaspoons (5 g) xanthan gum
- 2 teaspoons (4 g) baking powder
- 2 Tablespoons (24 g) granulated erythritol
- 2 eggs

For the filling -

- 1/4 cup (60 ml) ghee, melted
- 4 Tablespoons (48 g) granulated erythritol
- 2 Tablespoons (12 g) ground cinnamon

For the frosting -

- 1/2 cup (120 ml) ghee
- 1 to 2 cups (192 g to 384 g) powdered erythritol, to taste
- 1/2 teaspoon (3 ml) vanilla extract
- 1/4 cup (60 ml) unsweetened almond milk *(plus additional, if needed)*

INSTRUCTIONS

1. Add the sugar, ghee, and almond milk to a glass bowl. Either melt over boiling water or in the microwave until the bowl is just warm to the touch. If you have a thermometer, the mixture should be around 100 to 110°F (38 to 43°C). Too hot and it will kill the yeast but too cold and it will not activate.

2. Add the yeast to the milk mixture and stir to combine. Set the bowl in a warm place for 10 minutes until the mixture is frothy and bubbly. *(If it does not froth, your yeast is either inactive. Discard the mixture, and start the process again.)*

3. Meanwhile, mix the flours, collagen, xanthan gum, baking powder, and 2 Tablespoons (24 g) granulated erythritol in a large bowl.

4. Add the active *(frothy)* yeast mixture to the bowl and combine. Add the eggs and apple cider vinegar to the bowl and combine to form a sticky dough.

5. Wrap a large cutting board in plastic wrap. Place the dough on top of the board and place an additional layer of plastic wrap over the dough. Roll out the dough between the layers of plastic wrap until it is about a 1/4-inch (6.35 mm) thick large rectangle.

6. Carefully remove the top layer of plastic wrap. Brush 1/4 cup (60 ml) melted ghee over the dough and evenly sprinkle with the granulated erythritol and cinnamon.

7. Use the bottom layer of plastic wrap to carefully roll the dough into a tight log. (Be sure not to roll the plastic into the roll.) Use a sharp knife to cut the log into 8 equal size rolls.

8. Place the rounds in a lightly greased baking pan or oven-proof skillet. Cover with a kitchen towel and place in a warm location to proof (or rise) for 1 hour. The dough should increase in size during this time.

9. When ready to cook, preheat the oven to 350°F (175°C). Place the proofed rolls in the oven and bake for 20 to 30 minutes until lightly golden. *(You may want to cover with foil halfway through the bake time if the rolls start to brown too quickly.)*

10. Remove the cinnamon rolls from the oven and let cool for about 10 minutes before frosting.

11. Make the frosting by beating the ghee, 1 cup (192 g) powdered erythritol, almond milk, and vanilla until light and fluffy. Add additional erythritol, to taste, and additional almond milk, if needed, to reach desired consistency.

12. Evenly spread the frosting over the cooled cinnamon rolls and serve.

*Sugar is necessary to activate the yeast but is consumed by the yeast. The sugar will not remain in the recipe.

Nutritional Data (estimates) - per serving: 1 roll per serving
Calories: 345   Fat: 34 g   Total Carbs: 8 g   Fiber: 2 g   Sugar: 4 g   Net Carbs: 6 g
Protein: 5 g

DAIRY-FREE CHEESY BISCUITS

Prep Time: 15 minutes
Cook Time: 15-17 minutes
Yield: 8 biscuits

INGREDIENTS
- 2 cups (240 g) almond flour
- 2 eggs, whisked
- 2 teaspoons (4 g) baking powder
- 1/4 cup (60 ml) ghee or coconut oil
- 1/4 cup (60 ml) coconut yogurt *(or coconut cream)*
- 2 Tablespoons (16 g) nutritional yeast
- Dash of salt

INSTRUCTIONS
1. Preheat oven to 350°F (175°C).
2. Mix all the ingredients together to form a dough.
3. Form the dough into 8 biscuits and place onto a parchment paper-lined tray.
4. Bake for 15-17 min until just slightly browned.

Nutritional Data (estimates) - per biscuit:
Calories: 230   Fat: 21 g   Total Carbs: 6 g   Fiber: 4 g   Sugar: 1 g   Net Carbs: 2 g
Protein: 8 g

THE BEST CHEWY CHOCOLATE CHIP COOKIES

Prep Time: 10 minutes
Cooking Time: 15 minutes
Yield: 8 servings

INGREDIENTS

- 1 cup (120 g) almond flour
- 3 Tablespoons (21 g) coconut flour
- 1 teaspoon (2 g) baking powder
- 1/4 cup (48 g) erythritol
- 1 Tablespoon (7 g) flax meal *(use a food processor, blender, or coffee grinder to grind flax seeds into flax meal)*
- 1/4 cup (40 g) sugar-free chocolate chips (e.g., Lily's)
- 1 egg, whisked
- 2 Tablespoons (30 ml) of coconut oil
- 2 Tablespoons (30 ml) of coconut cream

INSTRUCTIONS

1. Preheat oven to 320°F (160°C).
2. Mix together all the ingredients to form a cookie dough.
3. Use a tablespoon to scoop up portions approximately 45 g in weight and form into 8 balls. Flatten and shape each ball into a cookie shape and place onto a baking tray lined with parchment paper.
4. Bake for around 15 minutes, rotating the tray after 8 minutes. Remove and allow to cool completely. Store in an airtight container.

Nutritional Data (estimates) - per cookie:
Calories: 146 Fat: 12 g Total Carbs: 4 g Fiber: 3 g Sugar: 1 g Net Carbs: 1 g
Protein: 4 g

LEMON POPPY SEED LOAF

Prep Time: 10 minutes
Cook Time: 40 minutes
Yield: 8 slices

INGREDIENTS

For the loaf -

- 3 cups (360 g) almond flour
- 1/2 cup (96 g) granulated erythritol
- 1 ½ Tablespoons (18 g) poppy seeds
- 2 teaspoons (4 g) baking powder
- 1/4 teaspoon (1 g) salt
- 4 medium eggs, lightly whisked
- 1/3 cup (80 ml) coconut oil, melted and cooled
- 2 Tablespoons (30 ml) unsweetened almond milk
- 3 Tablespoons (45 ml) lemon juice
- 1 Tablespoon (18 g) lemon zest
- 1 teaspoon (5 ml) vanilla extract

For the lemon glaze -

- 1/2 cup (72 g) powdered erythritol
- 1 Tablespoon (15 ml) lemon juice (*or to taste*)
- 1 teaspoon (6 g) lemon zest (*or to taste*)

INSTRUCTIONS

1. Preheat the oven to 375°F (190°C). Grease or line a 9-inch by 5-inch (*23 cm by 13 cm*) loaf pan with parchment paper and set aside.
2. In a large bowl, combine the almond flour, granulated erythritol, poppy seeds, baking powder and salt.
3. Add the remaining loaf ingredients to the bowl and combine to make a smooth batter. Pour the batter into the prepared loaf pan.
4. Place the loaf pan in the oven and bake for 40-50 minutes until cooked through and a toothpick inserted in the center comes out clean. (*Check after 20 minutes and cover with aluminum foil for the remaining cook time if the top of the loaf is browning too quickly.*)
5. Remove from the oven and let cool for about 15 minutes before removing the loaf from the pan and transferring to a wire rack to cool completely.
6. Meanwhile, whisk to combine the glaze ingredients. Prick the top of the cooled loaf with a toothpick and evenly drizzle the glaze on top.
7. Let the loaf sit for 2 to 3 minutes to partially absorb the glaze before slicing and serving.

Nutritional Data (estimates) :
Calories: 263   Fat: 24 g   Total Carbs: 7 g   Fiber: 4 g   Sugar: 2 g   Net Carbs: 3 g
Protein: 9 g

Chapter 4:

GAME NIGHT

MARGHERITA PIZZA

Prep Time: 15 minutes
Cook Time: 30 minutes
Yield: 4 servings

INGREDIENTS

- 1 keto almond flour pizza base
- 4 Tablespoons (60 ml) keto pizza sauce
- 4 Tablespoons (60 ml) keto cashew cheese *(or use cashew or almond butter)*
- 6 Basil leaves
- 1 Tablespoon (15 ml) olive oil

For the crust -
- 1/2 cup (60 g) almond flour
- 2 Tablespoons (14 g) flax meal
- 1 Tablespoon (2 g) nutritional yeast *(optional)*
- 1 Tablespoons (15 ml) olive oil
- 1 egg
- Salt and pepper, to taste

For the pizza sauce -
- 1 8-oz (225 g) can tomato sauce
- 1 6-oz (170 g) can tomato paste
- 2 teaspoons Italian seasoning
- Dash of garlic powder
- Dash of onion powder
- Salt and pepper, to taste

For the cashew cheese -
- 1 cup (4 oz or 120 g) raw cashews
- 3 Tablespoons (45 ml) coconut oil
- 1/4 cup (60 ml) water
- Dash of salt

INSTRUCTIONS

1. Preheat oven to 400°F (200°C).
2. Mix all the base ingredients together to form a dough. Roll out into a round flat pizza crust.
3. Bake for 15 minutes. Flip and then bake for another 5 minutes.
4. Top with the pizza sauce and cashew cheese.
5. Place back in the oven at 450°F (230°C) for 5-10 minutes until the cheese is browned.
6. Top with basil leaves and a few drizzles of olive oil.

Nutritional Data (estimates) - per serving:
Calories: 207   Fat: 18 g   Total Carbs: 7 g   Fiber: 3 g   Sugar: 2 g   Net Carbs: 4 g
Protein: 7 g

JALAPEÑO MUFFINS

Prep Time: 10 minutes
Cook Time: 20 minutes
Yield: 12 muffins

INGREDIENTS

- 3/4 cup (90 g) almond flour
- 1/4 cup (30 g) coconut flour
- 2 teaspoons (8 g) baking powder
- Dash of salt
- Small amount of stevia or erythritol
- 2 Tablespoons (30 ml) ghee or coconut oil, melted but not hot
- 3 eggs, whisked
- 3/4 cup (180 ml) coconut milk
- 4 jalapeño peppers (56 g), deseeded and finely diced

INSTRUCTIONS

1. Preheat oven to 350°F (175°C).
2. Place all the dry ingredients into a large mixing bowl and mix together.
3. Then add in the ghee or coconut oil, whisked eggs, and coconut milk.
4. Lastly, carefully stir in the chopped jalapeño pepper pieces.
5. Pour the mixture into a greased muffin tray or use muffin liners *(makes 12 muffins)*.
6. Bake for 18-20 minutes until a toothpick inserted into the middle of a muffin comes out clean.

Nutritional Data (estimates) - per muffin:
Calories: 96   Fat: 8 g   Total Carbs: 2 g   Fiber: 2 g   Sugar: 1 g   Net Carbs: 0 g
Protein: 3 g

ZUCCHINI FRIES

Prep Time: 10 minutes
Cook Time: 30 minutes
Yield: 6 servings

INGREDIENTS

- 5 zucchinis
- 1 cup (112 g) coconut flour
- 2 Tablespoons (14 g) onion powder
- 2 Tablespoons (20 g) garlic powder
- 2 teaspoons (4 g) paprika
- 2 teaspoons (4 g) chili powder
- 1 teaspoon (5 g) salt
- Black pepper, to taste

INSTRUCTIONS

1. Preheat oven to 400°F (200°C).
2. Cut zucchini ensuring the inner fleshy parts are mostly removed and discarded. Then slice the zucchini into 1/4-inch sticks.
3. Combine the coconut flour, onion powder, garlic powder, paprika, chili powder, salt, and freshly ground black pepper in a large bowl. Add the zucchini sticks to the bowl and toss to coat evenly.
4. Spread the sticks evenly on a greased baking tray and cook in the oven for 20 minutes.
5. Shake the tray and cook for an additional 5-10 minutes until golden.

Nutritional Data (estimates) - per serving:
Calories: 101   Fat: 2 g   Total Carbs: 15 g   Fiber: 8 g   Sugar: 5 g   Net Carbs: 7 g
Protein: 4 g

ASIAN CHICKEN WINGS

Prep Time: 10 minutes
Cook Time: 35 minutes
Yield: 5 servings

INGREDIENTS

- 2 lbs (900 g) chicken wings (approx. 10 wings), with skin on
- 2 Tablespoons (30 ml) sesame oil
- 1/4 cup (60 ml) gluten-free tamari sauce or coconut aminos
- 1 Tablespoon (6 g) ginger powder
- 2 teaspoons (10 ml) white wine vinegar
- 3 cloves of garlic, peeled and minced
- 1 teaspoon (5 g) sea salt

INSTRUCTIONS

1. Preheat oven to 400°F (200°C).
2. In a large container toss the sesame oil, tamari sauce, ginger powder, vinegar, garlic, and salt.
3. Whisk to thoroughly combine all ingredients. Add the chicken wings to the mixture.
4. Place the wings (meaty side up) on a parchment paper-lined baking sheet.
5. Bake for 30-35 minutes until the skin is crispy. *(Drizzle leftover marinade on the wings halfway through.)*
6. Turn on the broiler for a few minutes if you want the wings crispier.

Nutritional Data (estimates) - per serving:
Calories: 277 Fat: 22 g Total Carbs: 1 g Fiber: 0 g Sugar: 0 g Net Carbs: 1 g
Protein: 18 g

BACON WRAPPED ASPARAGUS

Prep Time: 10 minutes
Cook Time: 30 minutes
Yield: 4 servings

INGREDIENTS

- 16 slices of bacon, raw
- 16 spears of asparagus

INSTRUCTIONS

1. Preheat oven to 400°F (200°C).
2. Wrap each slice of bacon tightly around each asparagus spear.
3. Place on a baking tray and bake for 15 minutes.
4. Use tongs to turn the pieces around and bake for another 10-15 minutes until the bacon starts to get crispy.
5. If the bacon isn't crispy enough to your liking then turn the broiler on and crisp up the bacon for a few minutes.

Nutritional Data (estimates) - per serving:
Calories: 524   Fat: 52 g   Total Carbs: 4 g   Fiber: 2 g   Sugar: 2 g   Net Carbs: 2 g
Protein: 12 g

BACON & CHICKEN JALAPEÑO POPPERS

Prep Time: 10 minutes
Cook Time: 50 minutes
Yield: 3 servings

INGREDIENTS

- 1 chicken breast (1/2 lb or 225 g), cut into 6 strips
- 6 slices of bacon, raw
- 3 jalapeño peppers, ribs and seeds removed and sliced in half

INSTRUCTIONS

1. Preheat oven to 350°F (175°C).
2. Line a baking tray with parchment paper.
3. Place one jalapeño half onto a strip of chicken and wrap both together with a slice of bacon. Place, with the bacon ends folded down, onto the lined baking tray.
4. Repeat with remaining chicken, peppers, and bacon.
5. Bake for around 50 minutes. Check the chicken is cooked through and bacon is slightly crispy.

Nutritional Data (estimates) - per serving:
Calories: 389   Fat: 33 g   Total Carbs: 1 g   Fiber: 0 g   Sugar: 0 g   Net Carbs: 1 g
Protein: 22 g

MEATBALL SLIDERS

Prep Time: 15 minutes
Cook Time: 20 minutes
Yield: 4 sliders

INGREDIENTS

For the meatballs -

- 1/2 lb (227 g) ground beef
- 2 Tablespoons (8 g) parsley, finely diced
- 1 teaspoon (3 g) garlic powder
- 1 teaspoon (2-3 g) onion powder
- Salt and pepper, to taste
- 2 Tablespoons (30 ml) coconut oil, to cook with

For the sauce -

- 1 tomato, diced

- 1 teaspoon (2 g) Italian seasoning
- Salt and pepper, to taste
- 2 Tablespoons (30 ml) avocado oil, to cook with

For the bread (make 2 batches) -

- 1/3 cup (35 g) almond flour
- 1/2 teaspoon (2 g) baking powder
- Dash of salt
- 1 egg, whisked
- 2 and 1/2 Tablespoons (37 ml) ghee or coconut oil

INSTRUCTIONS

For the bread -

1. Whisk all the ingredients together in a mixing bowl.
2. Pour mixture into mug or microwaveable container.
3. Microwave for 90 seconds on high (this time may vary depending on your microwave).
4. Let cool, remove from mug, and slice into 4 slices.
   (Repeat steps above for a second batch)

For the meatballs and sauce -

1. Mix all the meatball ingredients together in a mixing bowl. Form small meatballs from the mixture and then fry in the coconut oil until cooked.
2. To make the sauce, add the avocado oil to a pan and sauté the tomatoes, Italian seasoning, and salt and pepper.
3. Put the sliders together by placing 4 small meatballs on a slice of bread, spooning some of the sauce on top and then placing the other slice of bread on top.

Nutritional Data (estimates) - per slider:
Calories: 483   Fat: 46 g   Total Carbs: 4 g   Fiber: 2 g   Sugar: 1 g   Net Carbs: 2 g
Protein: 16 g

BAKED CHICKEN NUGGETS

Prep Time: 15 minutes
Cook Time: 30 minutes
Yield: 6 servings

INGREDIENTS

- 2 chicken breasts (approx 4-5 oz/113-140 g), chopped into 2-inch by 1-inch chunks
- 2 eggs, whisked
- 1 cup (120 g) almond flour
- 2 Tablespoons (14 g) onion powder
- 2 Tablespoons (20 g) garlic powder
- 1 teaspoon (1 g) dried oregano
- 1 teaspoon (2 g) paprika powder
- 1 teaspoon (5 g) salt
- 1/2 teaspoon (1 g) black pepper

INSTRUCTIONS

1. Preheat oven to 350°F (175°C).
2. Add all the dry ingredients together into a large bowl. Mix well.
3. Place the eggs into a separate bowl.
4. Dip each chicken piece into the egg wash and then into the dry ingredients.
5. Place the chicken nuggets onto a greased baking tray and bake for 30 minutes until cooked and golden on the outside.

Nutritional Data (estimates) - per serving:
Calories: 259   Fat: 16 g   Total Carbs: 7 g   Fiber: 3 g   Sugar: 2 g   Net Carbs: 4 g
Protein: 21 g

PIZZA MEATBALL BITES

Prep Time: 10 minutes
Cook Time: 15 minutes
Yield: 4 servings

INGREDIENTS

- 1/4 lb (110 g) prosciutto or bacon
- 1/4 onion
- 1 lb (450 g) ground pork *(or chicken)*
- 10 black olives, pits removed
- 10 basil leaves
- 1 Tablespoon (8 g) nutritional yeast flakes
- Salt and pepper, to taste
- 2 Tablespoons (30 ml) keto pizza sauce

INSTRUCTIONS

1. Preheat oven to 400°F (200°C).
2. Food process all the ingredients together well.
3. Form small meatballs from the ingredients.
4. Place on a parchment paper-lined baking tray and bake for 15 minutes, turning after 10 minutes.
5. Place cocktail sticks into the meatballs.

Nutritional Data (estimates) - per serving:
Calories: 277   Fat: 18 g   Total Carbs: 2 g   Fiber: 0 g   Sugar: 1 g   Net Carbs: 2 g
Protein: 27 g

BASIC PORK RIND

Prep Time: 20 minutes
Cook Time: 2 hours 10 minutes
Yield: 4 servings

INGREDIENTS
- 1 large piece of pork skin *(approx. 2.2 lbs or 1 kg)*
- Salt and spices of choice *(suggestion – Chinese five spices)*

INSTRUCTIONS
1. Preheat the oven to 250°F (120°C). If your oven doesn't go down to this low of a temperature, set it to its lowest temperature and then open the oven door a crack.
2. Use a very sharp knife to remove all the fat from the skin.
3. You should be left with only the transparent skin.
4. Pat both sides dry and trim into smaller pieces *(approx. 1-inch by 1-inch or 2.5 cm by 2.5 cm)*.
5. Salt the pieces well and place on a wire rack placed over a tray. Place in the oven for 2 hours to dry out.
6. Remove the tray from the oven and transfer the pieces onto a clean tray.
7. Increase the temperature of the oven to max 440°F (230°C).
8. Once at temperature, place the tray into the oven and cook for 5-10 minutes allowing them to pop. *(Alternatively, you can pop the pork rinds by shallow frying them for 3-5 minutes in olive oil, lard, coconut oil or avocado oil.)*
9. Season with salt and spices of your choosing.
10. Allow to cool completely before storing in a sealed container. Makes approx. 30-50 pieces.

Nutritional Data (estimates) - per serving:
Calories: 152   Fat: 9 g   Total Carbs: 0 g   Fiber: 0 g   Sugar: 0 g   Net Carbs: 0 g
Protein: 17 g

ONION RINGS

Prep Time: 5 minutes
Cook Time: 4-5 minutes
Yield: 2 servings

INGREDIENTS

- 2.1 oz (59 g) pork rinds
- 1 Tablespoon (7 g) coconut flour
- 1 medium egg (44 g), beaten
- Oil, for deep-frying
- 1 large onion (110 g), peeled and cut into rings
- Salt and freshly ground black pepper
- Chopped parsley, to garnish

INSTRUCTIONS

1. Blitz the pork rinds into crumbs and place into a bowl.
2. Add the coconut flour into a second bowl and the beaten egg in a third bowl.
3. Heat enough oil in a pan to deep fry the onions. Working in batches, dip the onion rings in the coconut flour and dust off any excess. Then dip them into the egg and allow excess egg to drip off. Finally, press the onion rings into the pork crumbs until well-coated.
4. Fry the rings in the hot oil for 4-5 minutes, using a slotted spoon to gently turn them in the oil. Remove and drain well.
5. Season with salt and freshly ground black pepper and garnish with chopped parsley before serving.

Nutritional Data (estimates) - per serving:
Calories: 277   Fat: 22 g   Total Carbs: 1 g   Fiber: 0 g   Sugar: 0 g   Net Carbs: 1 g
Protein: 18 g

Chapter 5:

EASY BITES

BUFFALO CAULIFLOWER BITES

Prep Time: 10 minutes
Cook Time: 25 minutes
Yield: 4 servings

INGREDIENTS

- 1 head (approx. 1.5 lb or 600 g) cauliflower, broken into small florets
- 3 Tablespoons (45 ml) avocado oil
- 2 teaspoons (7 g) garlic powder
- 1 teaspoon salt (5 g) or to taste
- 2 Tablespoons (30 ml) ghee, melted
- 1/4 cup (60 ml) hot sauce

INSTRUCTIONS

1. Preheat oven to 450°F (230°C).
2. In a large mixing bowl, combine the avocado oil, garlic powder, and salt.
3. Toss the cauliflower florets in the mixture.
4. Place the cauliflower florets on a baking sheet and bake for 15 minutes.
5. Meanwhile, melt the ghee and combine with the hot sauce.
6. Toss the cauliflower florets in the hot sauce mixture and bake for another 5-10 minutes until slightly browned.
7. Serve with the **herb ranch dip** *(see recipe on **page 39**).*

Nutritional Data (estimates) - per serving:
Calories: 189   Fat: 18 g   Total Carbs: 8 g   Fiber: 4 g   Sugar: 4 g   Net Carbs: 4 g
Protein: 3 g

ZUCCHINI FRITTERS

Prep Time: 10 minutes
Cook Time: 20 minutes
Yield: 2 servings

INGREDIENTS

- 4 zucchinis, grated
- 2 green onions (10 g), diced
- 2 Tablespoons (14 g) onion powder
- 2 Tablespoons (20 g) garlic powder
- 2 teaspoons (2 g) dried oregano
- 3/4 cup (84 g) coconut flour
- 2 eggs, whisked
- 1/4 cup (60 ml) olive oil or avocado oil, to cook with
- Salt and freshly ground black pepper, to taste

INSTRUCTIONS

1. Preheat the oven to 350°F (175°C).
2. After grating or food processing the zucchini, squeeze out as much moisture as you can by wrapping it in muslin and squeezing as hard as you can. Squeeze until you have a dry pulp.
3. Combine all the ingredients except the olive oil. Form into 12 balls of approximately 1 oz (30 g) each. Then press into flat patties.
4. Heat the olive oil in a frying pan and carefully place the fritters into the hot oil. Once the bottom is golden and crispy, turn them over and cook for a few more minutes until that side is also browned.
5. Then, transfer the fritters to a greased baking tray and bake in oven for 10-15 minutes until fully cooked.

Nutritional Data (estimates) - per serving:
Calories: 181 Fat: 12 g Total Carbs: 12 g Fiber: 6 g Sugar: 4 g Net Carbs: 6 g
Protein: 5 g

CURRY CANDIED BACON

Prep Time: 5 minutes
Cook Time: 20 minutes
Yield: 4 servings

INGREDIENTS
- 8 slices of bacon, raw
- 2 Tablespoons (24 g) erythritol
- 1 Tablespoon (7 g) curry powder

INSTRUCTIONS
1. Preheat oven to 400°F (200°C).
2. Lay the bacon slices on a baking rack.
3. Mix the curry powder with the erythritol and rub over the bacon slices.
4. Bake the bacon until crispy *(approx. 20 minutes)*.
5. Enjoy as entire slices or crumble into small pieces for a snack.

Nutritional Data (estimates) - per serving:
Calories: 261   Fat: 26 g   Total Carbs: 1 g   Fiber: 1 g   Sugar: 0 g   Net Carbs: 0 g
Protein: 6 g

SPICY ROAST BEEF SALSA ROLL-UPS

Prep Time: 5 minutes
Cook Time: 0 minutes
Yield: 8 servings

INGREDIENTS

- 8 slices of deli roast beef *(or use deli ham or turkey or smoked salmon slices)*
- 1 avocado (approx. 1/2 lb or 225 g), stone removed and flesh mashed

For the salsa -
- 1 small tomato, finely diced
- 1/2 small red onion, finely diced
- 1 chili pepper, deseeded and finely chopped *(optional)*
- Zest and juice of 1/2 lime
- 1 Tablespoon (15 ml) olive oil
- Salt and pepper, to taste

INSTRUCTIONS

1. Make the salsa by tossing all the salsa ingredients together. Pour out excess liquid from the salsa.
2. Spread mashed avocado on each roast beef slice. And then spoon some salsa on top and roll up.

Nutritional Data (estimates) - per serving:
Calories: 88   Fat: 6 g   Total Carbs: 3 g   Fiber: 2 g   Sugar: 1 g   Net Carbs: 1 g
Protein: 6 g

CAJUN ROASTED ALMONDS

Prep Time: 5 minutes
Cook Time: 30 minutes
Yield: 4 servings

INGREDIENTS

- 2 cups (10 oz or 280 g) raw almonds *(or other nuts of your choosing)*
- 2 Tablespoons (30 ml) avocado oil
- 1 Tablespoon (6 g) paprika
- 2 teaspoons (7 g) garlic powder
- 1 teaspoon (3 g) onion powder
- 1 teaspoon (2 g) black pepper
- 1 teaspoon (2 g) cayenne pepper
- 2 teaspoons (10 g) salt

INSTRUCTIONS

1. Preheat oven to 300°F (150°C).
2. Toss the almonds with the avocado oil, spices, and salt in a small mixing bowl.
3. Place almonds on a parchment paper-lined baking tray and bake for 30 minutes until slightly browned.
4. Let cool and store in airtight container.

Nutritional Data (estimates) - per serving:
Calories: 175   Fat: 18 g   Total Carbs: 7 g   Fiber: 3 g   Sugar: 0 g   Net Carbs: 4 g
Protein: 5 g

BACON & CHICKEN OMELET BITES

Prep Time: 15 minutes
Cook Time: 30 minutes
Yield: 12 servings

INGREDIENTS

- 1 chicken breast (1/2 lb or 225 g), diced
- 12 slices of bacon, cooked and broken into bits
- 8 eggs, whisked
- 1 medium bell pepper, diced
- 1/2 medium onion, diced

INSTRUCTIONS

1. Preheat oven to 350°F (175°C).
2. Line a muffin tray with liners or grease well or use a silicone muffin tray.
3. Cook the bacon and then cook the diced chicken breast in the leftover bacon fat. Let cool for a few minutes.
4. In a large bowl, combine the whisked eggs, bell pepper, onion, cooked chicken and bacon together.
5. Spoon the mixture into the muffin trays (makes 12 muffins) and bake for 30 minutes.

Nutritional Data (estimates) - per serving:
Calories: 206   Fat: 17 g   Total Carbs: 1 g   Fiber: 0 g   Sugar: 0 g   Net Carbs: 1 g
Protein: 11 g

BACON STUFFED MUSHROOMS

Prep Time: 10 minutes
Cook Time: 25 minutes
Yield: 4 servings

INGREDIENTS

- 20 medium white button mushrooms
- 4 slices of bacon, raw
- 1/4 onion
- 2 Tablespoons (30 ml) olive oil or avocado oil

INSTRUCTIONS

1. Preheat oven to 400°F (200°C).
2. Clean the mushrooms *(remove the stems carefully with your hands – they should pop and then come out cleanly after you wriggle it a bit)*.
3. In the food processor, food process the bacon, onion, and mushroom stems to form a mince.
4. Heat up a frying pan, add in the oil and fry the mince until slightly browned.
5. Using your hands and a small spoon, stuff the bacon mixture into the mushrooms.
6. Place mushrooms onto a baking tray and bake for 15-20 minutes until slightly browned.

Nutritional Data (estimates) - per serving:
Calories: 200   Fat: 20 g   Total Carbs: 2 g   Fiber: 1 g   Sugar: 1 g   Net Carbs: 1 g
Protein: 5 g

CAULIFLOWER PATTIES

Prep Time: 10 minutes
Cook Time: 45 minutes
Yield: 4 servings

INGREDIENTS

- 1 head (approx. 1.5 lb or 600 g) cauliflower, broken into florets
- 2 eggs, whisked
- 1 cup (120 g) almond flour
- 1 Tablespoon (15 ml) coconut oil, for greasing baking tray
- Salt and pepper, to taste

INSTRUCTIONS

1. Preheat oven to 350°F (175°C).
2. Steam the cauliflower florets until softened.
3. Drain well and then food process or blend the cauliflower with the eggs and almond flour. Season with salt and pepper.
4. Form 8 patties. Place on a greased baking tray and bake for 30 minutes until slightly browned.

Nutritional Data (estimates) - per serving:
Calories: 234   Fat: 18 g   Total Carbs: 13 g   Fiber: 7 g   Sugar: 5 g   Net Carbs: 6 g
Protein: 11 g

MEXICAN LIME AND CHILI CUCUMBERS

Prep Time: 2 minutes
Cook Time: 0 minutes
Yield: 4 servings

INGREDIENTS

- 2 large cucumbers, cut into large wedges *(best chilled)*
- 1/4 cup (56 g) cashews
- 3 Tablespoons (45 ml) olive oil
- Zest and juice of 1 lime
- 1 teaspoon (2 g) chili powder
- Salt and pepper, to taste

INSTRUCTIONS

1. Toss all the ingredients together.

Nutritional Data (estimates) - per serving:
Calories: 151   Fat: 14 g   Total Carbs: 5 g   Fiber: 1 g   Sugar: 2 g   Net Carbs: 4 g
Protein: 3 g

SMOKEY BACON MEATBALLS

Prep Time: 15 minutes
Cook Time: 30 minutes
Yield: 8 servings

INGREDIENTS
- 2 chicken breasts or 1 lb (450 g) ground chicken
- 8 slices of bacon, cooked and crumbled
- 1 egg, whisked
- 2 cloves of garlic, peeled
- 1 Tablespoon (7 g) onion powder
- 2 drops of liquid smoke
- 4 Tablespoons (60 ml) avocado or olive oil, to cook with

INSTRUCTIONS
1. Place everything *(except the oil)* into a food processor and mix well.
2. From the mixture, form 20-24 small meatballs.
3. Place the oil into a large frying pan, and fry the meatballs until the meat is cooked *(cook one side for 5 minutes until browned, then flip and cook the other side for 5-10 minutes until done)*. You will probably need to cook them in a few batches.

Nutritional Data (estimates) - per serving:
Calories: 279   Fat: 25 g   Total Carbs: 1 g   Fiber: 0 g   Sugar: 0 g   Net Carbs: 1 g
Protein: 13 g

ZUCCHINI BACON BITES

Prep Time: 5 minutes
Cook Time: 35 minutes
Yield: 4 servings

INGREDIENTS

- 2 zucchinis, cut into 8 strips
- 8 thin slices of bacon, raw
- 2 Tablespoons (30 ml) olive oil
- 1 teaspoon (2 g) chili powder
- 1 teaspoon (3 g) garlic powder
- Salt and pepper, to taste

INSTRUCTIONS

1. Preheat oven to 350°F (175°C).
2. Place the zucchini strips into large mixing bowl and toss with olive oil, chili powder, garlic powder, salt and pepper.
3. Wrap a slice of bacon around each zucchini strip and place on a parchment paper-lined baking tray.
4. Bake for 35 minutes.
5. If you want the bacon crisper, place under the broiler for 3-5 minutes. Remove from oven and let cool slightly before serving.

Nutritional Data (estimates) - per serving:
Calories: 325   Fat: 33 g   Total Carbs: 2 g   Fiber: 1 g   Sugar: 1 g   Net Carbs: 1 g
Protein: 7 g

PAPRIKA DEVILED EGGS

Prep Time: 5 minutes
Cook Time: 10 minutes
Yield: 4 servings

INGREDIENTS
- 8 eggs
- 1/4 cup (60 ml) **keto mayo** *(see recipe on **page 32**)*
- 2 teaspoons (10 ml) mustard
- 1 teaspoon (5 ml) lemon juice or white wine vinegar
- 1 teaspoon (2 g) smoked paprika, for sprinkling
- Salt and pepper, to taste

INSTRUCTIONS
1. Hard boil the eggs.
2. Slice in half lengthwise with a sharp knife.
3. Carefully remove the egg yolks and mash them with keto mayo, mustard, lemon juice or vinegar, salt, and pepper.
4. Spoon the mixture back into the egg whites.
5. Sprinkle with smoked paprika.

Nutritional Data (estimates) - per serving:
Calories: 226   Fat: 20 g   Total Carbs: 0 g   Fiber: 0 g   Sugar: 0 g   Net Carbs: 0 g
Protein: 12 g

BAKED SCOTCH EGGS

Prep Time: 15 minutes
Cooking Time: 30 minutes
Yield: 6 servings

INGREDIENTS
- 6 hard-boiled eggs, peeled
- 1 lb (450 g) ground pork sausage with casings removed *(or use ground pork with 1 Tablespoon (3 g) Italian seasoning)*
- 1/4 cup (30 g) almond flour
- 2 Tablespoons (14 g) flax or chia seeds, ground into a meal *(use a food processor, blender, or coffee grinder)*
- 2 Tablespoons (30 ml) olive or avocado oil
- Salt and black pepper, to taste

INSTRUCTIONS
1. Preheat oven to 350°F (175°C).
2. In a small bowl, stir together the pork, almond flour, flax/chia meal, olive oil, salt and pepper.
3. Divide the meat mixture into 6 portions and flatten into patties and wrap around the boiled eggs, covering each egg completely. *(Add additional olive oil or a bit of water to help the mixture stick together if needed.)* Use some plastic wrap to help you get the mixture tightly around the boiled eggs.
4. Place on parchment paper-lined baking trays and bake for 15 minutes. Then turn the eggs over carefully and bake for another 15 minutes, or until sausage is cooked through. Remove from oven and let cool.

Nutritional Data (estimates) - per serving:
Calories: 198   Fat: 11 g   Total Carbs: 2 g   Fiber: 1 g   Sugar: 0 g   Net Carbs: 1 g
Protein: 24 g

CURRIED EGGS

Prep Time: 15 minutes
Cook Time: 5 minutes
Yield: 3 servings

INGREDIENTS

- 6 eggs
- 2 Tablespoons (30 ml) coconut oil, to cook with
- 2 cloves of garlic, peeled and minced
- 1 Tablespoon (7 g) curry powder
- 1 teaspoon (5 g) salt or to taste

INSTRUCTIONS

1. Hard boil the eggs.
2. Make a few slits in the eggs.
3. Place the coconut oil into a frying pan on medium heat.
4. Add in the garlic, curry powder, salt, and the eggs.
5. Fry for 2-3 minutes until the eggs are coated in the curry mixture.

Nutritional Data (estimates) - per serving:
Calories: 215   Fat: 17 g   Total Carbs: 2 g   Fiber: 1 g   Sugar: 0 g   Net Carbs: 1 g
Protein: 12 g

BEEF JERKY

Prep Time: 10 minutes + overnight
Cook Time: 8-10 hours
Yield: approx. 35 servings

INGREDIENTS

- 2.2 lbs (1 kg) of beef roast, fat trimmed
- 1/4 cup (60 ml) vinegar of your choice
- 2 Tablespoons (14 g) onion powder
- 2 Tablespoons (20 g) garlic powder
- 1 teaspoon (1 g) ground coriander
- 2 Tablespoons (30 g) salt
- 1 Tablespoon (1 g) coriander seeds, crushed
- 3 Tablespoons (45 ml) gluten-free tamari sauce or coconut aminos
- Black pepper, to taste

INSTRUCTIONS

1. Cut beef into 1-inch thick pieces along the grain. Pour vinegar into a bowl then dip each piece of raw meat in it. Allow the excess vinegar to stop dripping, then place the piece on a cooling rack set over a tray. Place the uncovered tray in the fridge overnight.
2. In a bowl, combine the onion powder, garlic powder, ground coriander, and salt, plus a generous sprinkle of black pepper. Partially crush the coriander seeds using a pestle and mortar and add to the mixture. Add the tamari sauce to form a paste.
3. Pat dry the meat then add to the bowl of paste. Massage the paste into each piece of meat.
4. Lay the pieces on a dehydrator set at 140°F (60°C) for 8-10 hours, depending on how moist you like the jerky. Turn them over occasionally.
5. Store in a sealed container.

Nutritional Data (estimates) - per serving:
Calories: 79   Fat: 6 g   Total Carbs: 1 g   Fiber: 0 g   Sugar: 0 g   Net Carbs: 1 g
Protein: 5 g

PHILLY ROLL

Prep Time: 5 minutes
Cook Time: 0 minutes
Yield: approx. 2 servings
Serving size: 1 roll

INGREDIENTS

- 2 slices smoked salmon *(approx. 2 oz or 56 g)*
- 1 oz (28 g) cashew cheese
- 6 thin slices of cucumber

INSTRUCTIONS

1. Place the smoked salmon slices on a piece of parchment paper. Spread 1/2 an ounce of cashew cheese on each slice of salmon. Top each with 3 thin slices of cucumber.
2. Roll up the salmon slices, starting at the bottom.

Nutritional Data (estimates) - per serving:
Calories: 111   Fat: 7 g   Total Carbs: 5 g   Fiber: 1 g   Sugar: 1 g   Net Carbs: 5 g
Protein: 8 g

FRIED "SPAGHETTI" FRITTERS

Prep Time: 15 minutes
Cook Time: 14 minutes
Yield: 8 servings

INGREDIENTS

- 1/2 large spaghetti squash (3 lb or 1.5 kg), seeds removed
- 2 eggs, whisked
- 3 Tablespoons (45 ml) olive oil
- 1 Tablespoon (3 g) Italian seasoning
- 1 Tablespoon (10 g) garlic powder
- 1 Tablespoon (7 g) onion powder
- Salt and black pepper, to taste

INSTRUCTIONS

1. Soften the spaghetti squash by placing it on a microwaveable plate *(cover with a paper towel)* and microwaving it for 8 minutes on high. When softened, you should be able to remove the strands easily with a fork. You can also bake the spaghetti squash, but it takes a lot longer to soften.
2. Remove the flesh and let cool for a few minutes before mixing with the eggs and all the seasoning.
3. Add the olive oil to a large frying pan over medium heat.
4. Using a large spoon, scoop squash mixture into the skillet and flatten slightly *(makes approx. 8 fritters)*. Cook for 3 minutes then carefully turn and cook for another 2-3 minutes.
5. Remove from pan and drain on paper towels. Enjoy.

Nutritional Data (estimates) - per serving:
Calories: 82   Fat: 6 g   Total Carbs: 5 g   Fiber: 1 g   Sugar: 2 g   Net Carbs: 4 g
Protein: 2 g

Chapter 6:
FROZEN DELIGHTS

BERRY FROZEN "YOGURT"

Prep Time: 5 minutes
Freezing Time: 30 minutes + 2 hours
Yield: 6 servings

INGREDIENTS

- 1 cup (70 g) mixed berries
- 1 cup (240 ml) coconut cream *(from the top of refrigerated cans of coconut milk)*
- 1 teaspoon (5 ml) vanilla extract
- Zest and juice of 1/2 lemon
- 2 Tablespoons (24 g) erythritol or stevia, to taste

INSTRUCTIONS

1. Mix together the vanilla, coconut cream, lemon, erythritol or stevia and freeze for 30 minutes.
2. Food process or blend the frozen coconut cream mixture and berries *(for a few pulses)*.
3. Divide between 6 small containers/glasses.
4. Place back into the freezer and freeze for 2+ hours. You may need to thaw it a bit before serving.

Nutritional Data (estimates) - per serving:
Calories: 117   Fat: 8 g   Total Carbs: 10 g   Fiber: 5 g   Sugar: 4 g   Net Carbs: 5 g
Protein: 0 g

BLUEBERRY POPSICLES

Prep Time: 10 minutes
Freezing Time: 4+ hours
Yield: 2 servings

INGREDIENTS
- 1/4 cup (48 g) blueberries
- 1/2 cup (120 ml) coconut milk
- Stevia or erythritol, to taste
- 1 Tablespoon (15 ml) lemon juice
- 1 teaspoon (5 ml) vanilla extract

INSTRUCTIONS
1. Blend all the ingredients together well.
2. Taste the mixture and add more of any ingredient you want.
3. Pour into ice pop molds *(this recipe makes approx. two 2.5 oz or 75 ml bars)*. Make sure there's a bit of space left over as the mixture will expand when it freezes.
4. Freeze for 4+ hours. When ready to eat, run the ice pop mold for a few minutes under hot water to make it easier to pull the ice pops out.

Nutritional Data (estimates) - per serving:
Calories: 112   Fat: 11 g   Total Carbs: 4 g   Fiber: 1 g   Sugar: 2 g   Net Carbs: 3 g
Protein: 1 g

FROZEN CHOCOLATE BERRIES

Prep Time: 5 minutes
Freezing Time: 2+ hours
Yield: 2 servings

INGREDIENTS

- 1 oz (30 g) 100% chocolate
- 5 raspberries
- 10 blueberries
- 1 teaspoon (5 ml) of almond butter *(optional)*

INSTRUCTIONS

1. Melt the dark chocolate in the microwave. This usually takes around 1 1/2 to 2 minutes.
2. Pour the chocolate into 2 muffin liners in a muffin tin.
3. Place the berries into the melted chocolate.
4. Finish by drizzling the almond butter over the top of the berries and chocolate. *(Makes 2 cups)*.
5. Freeze for 2+ hours.

Nutritional Data (estimates) - per serving:
Calories: 96   Fat: 4 g   Total Carbs: 5 g   Fiber: 2 g   Sugar: 2 g   Net Carbs: 3 g
Protein: 2 g

VANILLA PECAN ICE CREAM

Prep Time: 15 minutes
Freezing Time: 2+ hours
Yield: 2 servings

INGREDIENTS

- 2 eggs
- 3 Tablespoons (36 g) erythritol *(or to taste)*
- 1/2 cup (120 ml) coconut cream *(from the top of refrigerated cans of coconut milk)*
- 2 Tablespoons (15 g) pecan pieces
- 2 teaspoons (10 ml) vanilla extract

INSTRUCTIONS

1. Separate the egg yolks from the whites.
2. Whisk the egg whites until they form stiff peaks. Whisk in the erythritol and coconut cream.
3. Then fold in the egg yolks, pecan pieces, and vanilla extract.
4. Pour into 2 small containers and freezer for 2+ hours.

Nutritional Data (estimates) - per serving:
Calories: 243   Fat: 22 g   Total Carbs: 3 g   Fiber: 2 g   Sugar: 1 g   Net Carbs: 1 g
Protein: 7 g

MINT CHOCOLATE CHIP ICE CREAM

Prep Time: 1 hour 40 minutes
Freezing Time: 0 minutes
Yield: 8 servings

INGREDIENTS

- 1.5 oz (45 g) of fresh mint, leaves only
- 2 cans (400 ml each) of full-fat coconut milk, room temperature
- 1 small avocado, peeled
- 1/4 cup (48 g) erythritol or stevia, to taste
- 1.4 oz (39 g) of 100% dark chocolate

INSTRUCTIONS

1. In a food processor or blender, blitz the mint leaves and avocado to a smooth puree and set aside.
2. Shake the coconut milk then pour into a large bowl. Whisk until there are no lumps, then whisk in the puree. Cover the bowl and let sit for 1 hour at room temperature.
3. Strain the mixture through a double layer of muslin into a large bowl. Discard the pulp. Whisk in the erythritol or stevia.
4. Pour the new mixture into the ice cream maker and churn according to your machine's instructions. Just before switching the machine off, add the chocolate.
5. Transfer the ice cream into a freezer container and store covered.

Nutritional Data (estimates) - per serving:
Calories: 248   Fat: 24 g   Total Carbs: 5 g   Fiber: 3 g   Sugar: 1 g   Net Carbs: 3 g   Protein: 2 g

FROZEN COCONUT LEMON MERINGUE FAT BOMBS

Prep Time: 20 minutes
Freezing Time: 4+ hours
Yield: 24 fat bombs

INGREDIENTS
- 4 egg yolks, whisked
- 2 lemons, juice and zest
- 1/2 cup (120 ml) water
- 1/2 cup (80 g) erythritol + stevia
- 2 Tablespoons (30 ml) coconut oil
- 1/2 cup (120 ml) coconut cream
- Dash of salt

INSTRUCTIONS
1. Add the lemon juice and zest to a small pan with the 1/2 cup of water.
2. Whisk together the egg yolks and sweetener and add to the pan on medium heat. Stir for a few minutes until it starts to thicken.
3. Remove from the heat and stir in the coconut oil, cream and dash of salt.
4. Pour into silicone molds or ice cube trays.
5. Freeze for 4+ hours.

Nutritional Data (estimates) - per fat bomb:
Calories: 32   Fat: 3 g   Total Carbs: 1 g   Fiber: 0 g   Sugar: 0 g   Net Carbs: 1 g
Protein: 1 g

Chapter 7:

OTHER DESSERTS

CHOCOLATE FUDGE

Prep Time: 10 minutes
Freezer Time: 1 hour
Yield: 12 servings

INGREDIENTS
- 4 oz (112 g) 100% dark chocolate
- 3/4 cup (175 ml) coconut butter
- 1 teaspoon (5 ml) vanilla extract
- Stevia or erythritol, to taste

INSTRUCTIONS
1. Melt the chocolate.
2. Melt the coconut butter.
3. Combine all the ingredients together in a bowl with a fork.
4. Pour into a silicone loaf pan or a parchment paper-lined pan.
5. Place into the fridge for 2+ hours or freezer for 1 hour until it's solidified.
6. Remove from the pan and cut into 12 pieces.

Nutritional Data (estimates) - per serving:
Calories: 158 Fat: 13 g Total Carbs: 4 g Fiber: 2 g Sugar: 1 g Net Carbs: 2 g
Protein: 2 g

COCONUT BUTTER PECAN FAT BOMB BITES

Prep Time: 10 minutes
Fridge Time: 20 minutes
Yield: 4 servings

INGREDIENTS

- 2 Tablespoons (30 g) coconut butter
- Dash of cinnamon powder
- Dash of ginger powder
- Dash of nutmeg powder
- Dash of cloves powder
- Stevia or erythritol, to taste
- 20 pecan halves (40 g)

INSTRUCTIONS

1. Warm the coconut butter so that it is softened.
2. Mix the coconut butter, cinnamon, ginger, nutmeg, cloves, and stevia together.
3. Using a teaspoon, place small scoops of the coconut butter mixture on top of each pecan half.
4. Place into the fridge to set for 20 minutes.

Nutritional Data (estimates) - per serving:
Calories: 160   Fat: 15 g   Total Carbs: 5 g   Fiber: 3 g   Sugar: 1 g   Net Carbs: 2 g
Protein: 2 g

COOKIE DOUGH FUDGE

Prep Time: 10 minutes
Freezer Time: 1 hour
Yield: 12 servings

INGREDIENTS

- 1 cup (240 ml) unsweetened cashew butter (*or nut butter, of choice*)
- 1/4 cup (60 ml) coconut oil
- 2 oz (56 g) 100% dark chocolate, chopped small (*plus additional for topping*)
- 1 Tablespoon (12 g) granulated erythritol (*or to taste*)
- 1/2 teaspoon (3 ml) vanilla extract
- Pinch of salt

INSTRUCTIONS

1. In a microwave-safe bowl, melt the cashew butter with the coconut oil.
2. Add the remaining ingredients to the bowl and stir well to combine.
3. Pour the fudge mixture into an 8-inch by 4-inch (*20 cm by 10 cm*) parchment paper-lined loaf pan. If desired, scatter additional dark chocolate pieces on top of the fudge, gently pressing into the fudge.
4. Place the pan in the freezer for 1 hour or until firm.
5. Remove from the pan and cut into 12 pieces.

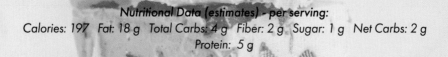

Nutritional Data (estimates) - per serving:
Calories: 197   Fat: 18 g   Total Carbs: 4 g   Fiber: 2 g   Sugar: 1 g   Net Carbs: 2 g
Protein: 5 g

PECAN CRISPS

Prep Time: 10 minutes
Cook Time: 10 minutes
Yield: 6 servings

INGREDIENTS

- 1 1/2 cups (150 g) pecans, chopped
- 12 pecan halves (24 g), for topping
- 1/4 cup (48 g) erythritol or stevia, to taste
- 1 egg, whisked
- 1/4 cup (30 g) flax or chia seed, ground into a meal in a blender or food processor or coffee grinder

INSTRUCTIONS

1. Preheat oven to 350°F (175°C).
2. Food process the 1.5 cups of pecans, erythritol, egg, and flax/chia meal together.
3. Place 12 muffin liners into a muffin pan.
4. Divide the mixture between the 12 muffin liners.
5. Bake for 8-10 minutes. Press a pecan half on top of each pecan crisp.
6. Remove from oven and let cool slightly before storing in an airtight container.

Nutritional Data (estimates) - per serving:
*Calories: 170 Fat: 14 g Total Carbs: 7 g Fiber: 4 g Sugar: 1 g Net Carbs: 3 g
Protein: 7 g*

MINI PECAN PIES

Prep Time: 15 minutes
Cook Time: 15 minutes
Yield: 6 servings

INGREDIENTS

For the crust -
- 1/2 cup (60 g) almond flour
- 1 egg, whisked
- 2 Tablespoons (14 g) flax meal *(use a food processor, blender, or coffee grinder to grind flax seeds into flax meal)*
- 2 Tablespoons (30 ml) ghee, melted but not too hot

For the filling -
- 1/2 cup (60 g) pecans, roughly chopped
- 1/4 cup (60 ml) ghee, melted but not too hot
- 1 egg, whisked
- 1/4 cup (48 g) granulated erythritol *(or stevia)*
- 1 teaspoon (5 ml) vanilla extract

INSTRUCTIONS

1. Preheat oven to 350°F (175°C).
2. Make the crust by mixing all the crust ingredients together. Press the dough into 6 mini muffin cups to form the crust.
3. Make the filling by mixing together all the filling ingredients in a bowl.
4. Pour into the 6 crusts.
5. Bake for 15 minutes until the pie crust is slightly golden.
6. Let cool then enjoy.

Nutritional Data (estimates) - per serving:
Calories: 243 Fat: 24 g Total Carbs: 4 g Fiber: 3 g Sugar: 1 g Net Carbs: 1 g
Protein: 6 g

PEPPERMINT PATTIES

Prep Time: 15 minutes
Freezer Time: 3 hours
Yield: 12 servings

INGREDIENTS

To make the peppermint filling -
- 1/2 cup (120 ml) coconut butter
- 1 Tablespoon (15 ml) coconut oil, melted
- 1 teaspoon (5 ml) peppermint extract
- 1/4 cup (48 g) eryrithol or stevia, to taste

To make the chocolate layer -
- 2 Tablespoons (60 ml) coconut oil, melted
- 4 oz (112 g) 100% dark chocolate

INSTRUCTIONS

1. In a bowl mix together all the peppermint filling ingredients.
2. Pour a small amount of the peppermint mixture into mini cupcake or muffin trays (*silicone ones work best for this*) to form a 1/3-inch (0.8 cm) thick layer. Freeze for 1 hour until solid.
3. Melt the dark chocolate and coconut oil together and combine. Make sure it's not too hot but still liquid.
4. Remove the solid peppermint fillings from the cups.
5. Pour a small amount of the chocolate mixture into each cup so that it covers the base, place the peppermint filling back into the cup and then cover with a bit more chocolate so that it's completely covered. Repeat for all the patties (*makes approx. 12 patties*).
6. Freeze for 2+ hours until solid. Thaw for 10 minutes before enjoying.

Nutritional Data (estimates) - per serving:
Calories: 153 Fat: 13 g Total Carbs: 3 g Fiber: 2 g Sugar: 1 g Net Carbs: 1 g
Protein: 2 g

PUMPKIN PIE

Prep Time: 10 minutes + cooling time
Cook Time: 15 minutes + 4 hours setting time
Yield: 1 pie (8 servings)

INGREDIENTS

To soak the cashew nuts -
- 1/2 cup (112 g) of unroasted cashew nuts

For the pumpkin spice -
- 1/2 Tablespoons (3 g) of cinnamon powder
- 1/2 teaspoon (1 g) of ginger powder
- Pinch ground cloves
- Pinch ground nutmeg

For the pastry case -
- 1 cup (120 g) of almond flour
- 1/4 cup (28 g) of ground flaxseed *(use a food processor, blender, or coffee grinder to grind flax seeds into flax meal)*
- 1/4 cup (28 g) of coconut flour
- 1/4 cup (60 ml) of water

For the filling -
- Reserved soaked cashew nuts
- 3.5 oz (98 ml) full-fat coconut milk
- 1 Tablespoon (6 g) powdered gelatin
- 2 Tablespoons (12 g) hot water
- 7 oz (197 g) pumpkin puree
- 1 1/2 teaspoon of reserved pumpkin spice
- 2.8 oz (78 g) erythritol

Nutritional Data (estimates) - per serving:
Calories: 210   Fat: 16 g   Total Carbs: 12 g   Fiber: 5 g   Sugar: 3 g   Net Carbs: 7 g
Protein: 7 g

INSTRUCTIONS

Prep -
1. Place the cashew nuts into a bowl and cover with hot water. Leave to soak overnight.

Make the crust -
2. Preheat oven to 350°F (175°C).
3. Mix together the almond flour, flaxseed, coconut flour, and quarter cup of water to form a dough. Press the dough into a greased pie dish.
4. Bake for 10-12 min until slightly browned. Remove and allow to cool.

Make the filling -
5. Drain the cashew nuts, keeping 1/4 cup of the water.
6. Place the soaked nuts and the 1/4 cup reserved water into a food processor.
7. Blitz well, stopping to scrape down the sides of the bowl regularly. Add the coconut milk and continue to blitz the mixture until completely smooth. Set aside.
8. Dissolve the gelatin in the hot water and set aside while you prepare the rest of the filling.
9. Add the pumpkin puree, pumpkin spice, and cashew nut mixture to a pan.
10. Cook over low to moderate heat for 2-3 minutes, stirring continuously. Add the erythritol and the gelatin mixture and stir well to combine.
11. Pour the filling into the cooled pie crust and place in the fridge to set for several hours.

JAFFA DARK CHOCOLATE MOUSSE

Prep Time: 10 minutes
Cook Time: 0 minutes
Yield: 6 servings

INGREDIENTS

- 2 ripe avocados (approx. 1 lb or 450 g), de-stoned and scoop out the flesh
- 3 Tablespoons (18 g) 100% cacao powder
- Zest of 1 navel orange
- Erythritol or stevia, to taste

INSTRUCTIONS

1. Blend everything together well. Taste the mousse and add more sweetener if needed.

Nutritional Data (estimates) - per serving:
Calories: 119   Fat: 10 g   Total Carbs: 7 g   Fiber: 5 g   Sugar: 0 g   Net Carbs: 2 g
Protein: 2 g

MCT LIME MINT GUMMY BEARS

Prep Time: 15 minutes
Cook Time: 15 minutes
Freezing/Refrigeration Time: 2+ hours
Yield: 8 servings

INGREDIENTS
- 1/4 cup (60 ml) fresh lime juice
- 2 Tablespoons (12 g) gelatin powder
- 2 Tablespoons (24 g) erythritol or stevia, to taste
- 2 drops of peppermint essence
- 1 teaspoon (5 g) MCT powder *(optional)*

INSTRUCTIONS
1. In a small saucepan, heat up the lime juice and slowly stir in the gelatin powder and erythritol so that it all dissolves.
2. Pour into silicone molds *(or ice-cube trays)*.
3. Freeze or refrigerate for 2+ hours.

Nutritional Data (estimates) - per serving:
Calories: 13   Fat: 1 g   Total Carbs: 1 g   Fiber: 0 g   Sugar: 1 g   Net Carbs: 1 g
Protein: 2 g

MINI COCONUT CREAM PIE

Prep Time: 20 minutes
Cook Time: 40 minutes
Yield: 4 mini pies
Serving size: 1 mini pie

INGREDIENTS

For the crust -

- 1 cup (120 g) almond flour
- 1/4 cup (28 g) flax meal *(use a food processor, blender, or coffee grinder to grind flax seeds into flax meal)*
- 1/4 cup (28 g) coconut flour
- 1/4 cup (60 ml) water

For the filling -

- 1/2 cup (40 g) shredded coconut
- 1/3 cup (80 ml) coconut cream
- 1 egg
- 2 Tablespoons (30 ml) ghee, melted
- 2 teaspoons (10 ml) vanilla extract
- Erythritol, to taste
- Dash of salt

INSTRUCTIONS

For the crust -

1. Preheat oven to 350°F (175°C).
2. Mix together all the ingredients to form a dough. Add additional water if needed to form the dough.
3. To make 4 small pie crusts, divide the dough into 4 pieces and roll each out into a flat circle. Then press each into greased small pie or tart pans.
4. If you're using this recipe to create one large pie, then don't divide the dough, and instead, roll the dough into a larger flat piece and place into a 9-inch pie tin.
5. Bake for 10-12 min until slightly browned.

For the filling -

1. Preheat oven to 325°F (160°C).
2. Combine the coconut cream, egg, ghee, vanilla extract, erythritol, and dash of salt. Fold in the shredded coconut.
3. Pour filling into the baked pie crusts.
4. Bake for 30 minutes until the fillings are set. Let cool and the store in fridge for 2 hours before serving.

Nutritional Data (estimates) - per serving:
Calories: 377 Fat: 33 g Total Carbs: 13 g Fiber: 9 g Sugar: 3 g
Net Carbs: 4 g Protein: 10 g

COOKIE BUTTER

Prep Time: 15 minutes
Cook Time: 15 minutes
Yield: 12 servings
Serving size: 2 Tablespoons

INGREDIENTS

- 1 3/4 cup (210 g) almond flour
- 1/2 cup (56 g) coconut flour
- 1 Tablespoon (6 g) ground cinnamon
- 1 1/2 teaspoons (3 g) ground ginger
- 1/2 teaspoon (1 g) allspice
- 1/2 teaspoon (1 g) baking powder
- Dash of salt
- 1/4 cup (48 g) erythritol
- 1/2 cup (120 ml) ghee
- 1 large egg, at room temperature
- 3/4 cup (180 ml) coconut oil, melted *(reserved for later use)*

INSTRUCTIONS

1. Preheat oven to 325°F (160°C). Line a baking sheet with parchment paper.
2. Mix all the ingredients together except for the coconut oil and mix well to form a dough.
3. Divide the dough into small even pieces. Flatten the pieces on the baking sheet.
4. Bake for 12-15 minutes, or until lightly browned on the top but still soft to the touch.
5. Allow the cookies to cool slightly.
6. Grab your high-speed blender and add about half of the melted coconut oil to the blender. Toss all of the cookies on top, and then add the remaining oil on top.
7. Blend on medium-high speed until the mixture forms a butter - a cookie butter!
8. Pour the butter into a glass container and store in the fridge for up to 10 days *(just bring to room temperature before serving)*.

Nutritional Data (estimates) - per serving:
Calories: 302   Fat: 31 g   Total Carbs: 5 g   Fiber: 3 g   Sugar: 1 g   Net Carbs: 2 g
Protein: 4 g

VANILLA FUDGE

Prep Time: 10 minutes
Freezer Time: 1 hour
Yield: 9 servings

INGREDIENTS

- 1/3 cup (80 ml) coconut cream (*from the top of refrigerated cans of coconut milk*)
- 1/4 cup (60 ml) coconut oil
- 1/3 cup (80 ml) unsweetened tahini (*or nut butter, of choice*)
- 1 Tablespoon (12 g) powdered erythritol (*or to taste*)
- 1 Tablespoon (6 g) almond flour
- 2 teaspoons (10 ml) vanilla extract
- Pinch of salt

INSTRUCTIONS

1. In a double boiler, gently melt the coconut cream with the coconut oil. (*Alternatively, fill a pot with 1-inch [2 ½ cm] of water and bring to a low simmer. Place the coconut cream and coconut oil in a bowl and place it in the pot, making sure the bowl doesn't touch the water.*) Once melted, remove from the heat and set aside to cool slightly.
2. Add the remaining ingredients to the coconut mixture and stir well to combine.
3. Pour the fudge mixture into a small parchment paper-lined rectangular pan.
4. Place the pan in the freezer for 1 hour or until firm.
5. Remove from the pan and cut into 9 pieces.

Nutritional Data (estimates) - per serving:
Calories: 124   Fat: 12 g   Total Carbs: 3 g   Fiber: 1 g   Sugar: 0 g   Net Carbs: 2 g
Protein: 2 g

LEMON DROP GUMMIES

Prep Time: 15 minutes
Cook Time: 15 minutes
Yield: 4 servings

INGREDIENTS

- 1/4 cup (60 ml) fresh lemon juice
- 2 Tablespoons (12 g) gelatin powder
- 2 Tablespoons (24 g) erythritol or stevia, to taste

INSTRUCTIONS

1. In a small saucepan, heat up the lemon juice and slowly stir in the gelatin powder and erythritol so that it all dissolves.
2. Pour into silicone molds *(or ice-cube trays)*.
3. Freeze or refrigerate for 2+ hours.

Nutritional Data (estimates) - per serving:
Calories: 15   Fat: 0 g   Total Carbs: 1 g   Fiber: 0 g   Sugar: 1 g   Net Carbs: 1 g
Protein: 3 g